INTRODUCTION TO THE WORLD'S MAJOR RELIGIONS

Introduction to the World's Major Religions

HINDUISM

Volume 6

Steven J. Rosen

Lee W. Bailey, General Editor

GREENWOOD PRESS
Westport, Connecticut • London

Library of Congress Cataloging-in-Publication Data
available on request from the Library of Congress.

British Library Cataloguing in Publication Data is available.

Copyright © 2006 by Steven J. Rosen

ISBN 0–313–33634–2 (set)
    0–313–33327–0 (vol. 1)
    0–313–32724–6 (vol. 2)
    0–313–33251–7 (vol. 3)
    0–313–32683–5 (vol. 4)
    0–313–32846–3 (vol. 5)
    0–313–33590–7 (vol. 6)

First published in 2006

Greenwood Press, 88 Post Road West, Westport, CT 06881
An imprint of Greenwood Publishing Group, Inc.
www.greenwood.com

Printed in the United States of America

The paper used in this book complies with the
Permanent Paper Standard issued by the National
Information Standards Organization (Z39.48–1984).

10 9 8 7 6 5 4 3 2 1

Introduction to the World's Major Religions
Lee W. Bailey, General Editor

Judaism, Volume 1
Emily Taitz

Confucianism and Taoism, Volume 2
Randall L. Nadeau

Buddhism, Volume 3
John M. Thompson

Christianity, Volume 4
Lee W. Bailey

Islam, Volume 5
Zayn R. Kassam

Hinduism, Volume 6
Steven J. Rosen

To my beti . . .
Aham tvam prinami

CONTENTS

SET FOREWORD

This set, *Introduction to the World's Major Religions,* was developed to fill a niche between sophisticated texts for adults and the less in-depth references for middle schoolers. It includes six volumes on religions from both Eastern and Western traditions: Judaism, Christianity, Islam, Hinduism, Confucianism and Taoism, and Buddhism. Each volume gives a balanced, accessible introduction to the religion.

Each volume follows a set format so readers can easily find parallel information in each religion. After a Timeline and Introduction, narrative chapters are as follows: the "History of Foundation" chapter describes the founding people, the major events, and the most important decisions made in the faith's early history. The "Texts and Major Tenets" chapter explains the central canon, or sacred texts, and the core beliefs, doctrines, or tenets, such as the nature of deities, the meaning of life, and the theories of the afterlife. The chapter on "Branches" outlines the major divisions of the religion, their reasons for being, their distinctive doctrines, their historical background, and structures today. The chapter on "Practice Worldwide" describes the weekly worship practices, the demographic statistics indicating the sizes of various branches of religions, the global locations, and historical turning points. The chapter on "Rituals and Holidays" describes the ritual practices of the religions in all their varieties and the holidays worldwide, such as the Birth of the Buddha, as they have developed historically. The chapter on "Major Figures" covers selected notable people in the history of each religion and their important influence. A glossary provides definitions for major special terms, and the index gives an alphabetic locator for major themes. A set index is included in volume 6 (to facilitate comparison).

In a world of about 6 billion people, today the religion with the greatest number of adherents is Christianity, with about 2 billion members, comprising 33 percent of the globe's population. Next largest is Islam, with about 1.3 billion members, (about 22 percent). Hindus number about 900 million (about 15 percent). Those who follow traditional Chinese religions number about 225 million (4 percent). Although China has the world's largest population, it is officially Communist, and Buddhism has been blended with traditional Confucianism and Taoism, so numbers in China are difficult to verify. Buddhism claims about 360 million members (about 6 percent of the world's population). Judaism, although historically influential, has a small number of adherents—about 14 million (0.2 percent of the world's population). These numbers are constantly shifting, because religions are always changing and various surveys define groups differently.[1]

Religions are important elements of the worldview of a culture. They express, for example, the cultural beliefs about cosmology, or picture of the universe (e.g., created by God or spontaneous), and the origin of humanity (e.g., purposeful or random), its social norms (e.g., monogamy or polygamy), its ways of relating to ultimate reality (e.g., sacrifice or obedience to law), the historical destiny (e.g., linear or cyclical), life after death (e.g., none or judgment), and ethics (e.g., tribal or universal).

As the world gets smaller with modern communications and global travel, people come in contact with those of other religions far more frequently than in the past. This can cause conflicts or lead to cooperation, but the potential for hostile misunderstanding is so great that it is important to foster knowledge and understanding. Noting parallels in world religions can help readers understand each religion better. Religions can provide ethical guidance that can help solve serious cultural problems. During war the political question "why do they hate us?" may have serious religious aspects in the answer. New answers to the question of how science and religion in one culture can be reconciled may come from another religion's approach. Scientists are increasingly analyzing the ecological crisis, but the solutions will require more than new technologies. They will also require ethical restraint, the motivation to change the destructive ecological habits of industrial societies, and some radical revisioning of worldviews. Other contemporary issues, such as women's rights, will also require patriarchal religions to undertake self-examination. Personal faith is regularly called into consideration with daily news of human destructiveness or in times of crisis, when the very meaning of life comes into question. Is life basically good? Will goodness in the big picture overcome immediate evil? Should horrendous behavior be forgiven? Are people alone in a huge, indifferent universe, or is the ultimate reality a caring, just power behind the scenes of human and cosmic history? Religions offer various approaches, ethics, and motivations to deal with such issues. Readers can use the books in this set to rethink their own beliefs and practices.

NOTE

1. United Nations, "Worldwide Adherents of All Religions by Six Continental Areas, Mid-2002," *World Population Prospects: The 1998 Revision* (New York: United Nations, 1999).

ACKNOWLEDGMENTS

In the Bhagavad Gita (7.7), Lord Krishna says that everything in creation rests on Him, just as pearls are strung on a thread. Similarly, numerous people have contributed pearl-like blessings on this work, without which it would merely be a naked string. These include Howard Resnick (Hriday-ananda Dasa Goswami), Alan Keislar, Jack Hawley, Michael Witzel, Thomas Gugler, Edwin Bryant, Luis Reimann, Bruce Sullivan, Joan Mencher, Vasudha Narayanan, Jan Brzezinski, Neal Delmonico, Graham Schweig, Joshua Greene, Fred Smith, Gavin Flood, Klaus Klostermaier, Nrisimhananda Prabhu, Yudhisthira Prabhu, Manikundala Ma, Giriraja Swami, Lomasha Rishidas, Hansa Medley, Nandini, Stacey Hlad, and Vatsal. In addition to these friends, who answered many of my questions and gave invaluable advice and other assistance as I worked on this book, I would like to thank Francis X. Clooney, who thought of me when Greenwood Press was looking for an author to do a volume on Hinduism. Friends like Francis are pearls indeed.

INTRODUCTION

Hinduism is among the oldest and most multifaceted of spiritual traditions. It can best be defined as a way of life based on the teachings of ancient wisdom texts, such as the Vedas and the Upanishads. Beyond this, however, the religion is difficult to define, chiefly because the word "Hinduism" does not refer to one particular religion but, rather, is a catchphrase for a group of religions, all with origins in India. These religions share certain underlying teachings, and for this reason they are all placed under the Hindu umbrella. The essential core of these religious traditions is properly referred to as Sanatana Dharma, which roughly translates as "eternal religion," and the words "Hindu" and "Hinduism" are foreign, not indigenous to India itself.[1]

The Hindu tradition is best understood when compared to a fruit tree, with its roots represented by the Vedas, the Upanishads, and other ancient scriptures. The large trunk of the tree is comparable to the spiritual experiences of numerous sages and saints, whose insights are honored as much as those of the sacred texts and, indeed, grow out of these texts. The branches are analogous to the religious traditions that sprout from these roots and its trunk. These are the specific religions that, together, are called Hinduism. Of all such religions the most prominent are Vaishnavism, which refers to the worship of Vishnu (the Supreme God), Shaivism, the veneration of Shiva (God when He manifests for the purpose of universal destruction), and Shaktism, reverence for the Goddess (the Mother of the universe).[2] There are many smaller branches as well, symbolizing various sects and subsects found in India. The fruits of this tree are the realizations one gets by practicing the various forms of Hindu religion; the topmost fruit is liberation, which begins with release from material conditioning and culminates in love of God.

Interestingly, Hinduism accommodates a good number of theological perspectives—with its various religions espousing monotheism, polytheism, pantheism, and so on, in diverse ways—and absorbs the perspectives of other religions as well. It is thus characterized by a rich variety of ideas and practices that cannot be confined by one particular doctrine. In fact, it is more defined by what a person does than by what he or she thinks. Hinduism is cultural, not doctrinal, taking its inspiration from the many traditions of its ancestors as opposed to any one teaching. It is so diverse in its underlying premises and practical manifestations that it has been called a living encyclopedia of religions.

This "encyclopedia" is now considered the world's third largest religion, after Christianity and Islam. It consists of more than 800 million people—almost 15 percent of the world's population—and that is just in India, the land of its birth. In the United States, there are more than 1 million Hindus, and there are several million more throughout the world.[3] This large number of Hindus worldwide, however, is somewhat misleading, for, as stated, Hinduism is a mélange of religions and not just one monolithic tradition. Vaishnavism—a religion centered on the monotheistic worship of Vishnu, "the all-pervasive Lord," a being who in Western religion might be called "God"—is the "Hindu" tradition with the largest number of adherents today. As such, it is often considered the core of modern Hinduism, and for this reason it is the focus of this volume, even if the other Hindu traditions will be represented here as well.[4]

WHAT IS HINDUISM?

All varieties of Hinduism share certain traits. Thus, according to expert consensus, a religion may properly be called a form of Hinduism if it has the following characteristics, or essential beliefs:

1. Belief in the divinity of the Vedas, the world's most ancient scripture, as well as faith in the "fifth Veda," or the epics and the Puranas, which are the main holy books of the Hindu religion
2. Belief in one, all-pervasive Supreme Reality, manifesting as both an impersonal force, which is called Brahman, and as a personal divinity (known variously, according to whichever particular tradition one adheres to)
3. Belief in the cyclical nature of the time—that there are world ages that repeat themselves like seasons

4. Belief in karma, the law of action and reaction, by which each person creates his or her own destiny
5. Belief in reincarnation—that the soul evolves through many births until all past deeds have been resolved, leading to ultimate liberation from the material world
6. Belief in alternate realities with higher beings—God and His manifold manifestations—who can be accessed through temple worship, rituals, sacraments, and prayer
7. Belief in enlightened masters, or gurus—exemplary souls who are fully devoted to God and who act as a conduit for others to reach Him
8. Belief in non-aggression and non-injury (*ahimsa*) as a way of showing love to all creatures. This includes the idea of the sacredness of all life and its concomitant universal compassion.
9. Belief that all revealed religions are essentially correct, as aspects of one ultimate reality, and that religious tolerance is the hallmark of true wisdom
10. Belief that the living being is first and foremost a spiritual entity, a soul within the body, and that the spiritual pursuit is consequently the essence and real purpose of life
11. Belief that an organic social system, traditionally called Varnashrama, is essential in the proper and effective functioning of humankind, and that this system should be based on intrinsic quality and natural aptitude as opposed to birthright.[5]

All forms of Hindu religion will not always demonstrate adherence to these principles to the same degree, or in the same way. The Varnashrama social system, to cite one example, is rigidly enforced by some Hindu traditions, while vehemently rebelled against in others. In either case, social status plays a central role in the Hindu mindset, whether the particular tradition accepts it or rejects it. The worshippers of Vishnu, to cite another example, are generally strict supporters of non-injury to sentient beings *(ahimsa)*, taking it to the point of vegetarianism. Shaktas, or worshippers of the Goddess, on the other hand, tend to deemphasize this principle and sometimes engage in animal sacrifices. Even here, the rationale for such sacrifices is replete with an *ahimsa* sensibility, explaining its related violence in terms of theological necessity and unfortunate concessions. Overall, however, the 11 principles outlined previously are found in all religions that call themselves Hindu, and so one *can* speak of an overarching Hindu tradition.

Sometimes this is taken too far, and clearly divergent religions are included under the general rubric of Hinduism. The contemporary Indian legal system, for example, deliberately subsumes Buddhism, Jainism, and

Sikhism, three other Eastern religions, under Hinduism's ever widening banner.[6] Such ambiguity in regard to the term *Hinduism* makes its usefulness a matter of debate. Indeed, only a few of these 11 principles are found in these three other religions.

THE ESSENCE OF RELIGIOUS DUTY

If the word "Hinduism" is too vague to be of much value, what *should* one call the many Hindu religions of India? Hindus themselves refer to their religion as Sanatana Dharma, or *eternal religion*, as mentioned previously. The central word here is *dharma*, which means "to support, hold up, or bear." In common parlance it means, "right way of living," "Divine Law," "path of righteousness," "faith," and "duty." It refers to the essence of religion.

The English word *religion*, however, is not exactly a synonym for *dharma*, although it is tempting to think of the words in this way. Religion conveys the idea of a faith that might one day change. For instance, one might believe in a specific religion at a particular point in one's life and then, after some time, believe in another, shifting from faith to faith. And there are various reasons one might do this, both legitimate and illegitimate. But Sanatana Dharma refers to that activity or function that cannot be changed. Heat and light, for example, are the *dharma* of fire; without heat and light, fire has no meaning. Similarly, state Hindu texts, each living entity has an essential purpose, a reason for being, and regardless of one's adopted or inherited faith, this is one's *dharma*, and it subsists, no matter what.

According to most forms of modern Hinduism, the inherent nature of the soul is to serve God. This is called the living being's essential *dharma*, or his eternal function. Entities in this world may have many secondary *dharmas*, but this is described as the central one. India's sacred texts explain that of the numberless souls who occupy the spiritual realm, or the kingdom of God, some shift in focus and fall into illusion; they undergo an unfortunate transformation of consciousness. These are the souls who come to the material world. Here their eternal function becomes distorted, and they find themselves no longer serving God directly. No more are they privy to their original *dharma*, their eternal function, and, instead, they become engaged in "unnatural" activity. Over the course of many lifetimes (for Hindu thought is always set against the backdrop of reincarnation, which is discussed at length in a later chapter), such activity becomes commonplace, and the soul forgets his original and natural function. Identity and nature are now thoroughly ensconced in an alien environment, and life in the material world becomes the only thing that seems real.

This distorted nature, however, is necessarily temporary. Be that as it may, it gradually takes prominence over the living being's true nature—his real *dharma*—and asserts its contrived features in his day-to-day life. The traditional example is water, whose real *dharma* is fluidity. When water transforms into ice, its *dharma*, or its original nature, also transforms. Its "new" *dharma* becomes hardness, as water solidifies. But this new hardened liquid is only a distorted facsimile, manifesting in place of water's real nature. Eventually, it becomes apparent that water in its hardened state is only temporary, for when the temperature again becomes warm, water will revert to its true nature, revealing its essential liquidity.

Hindu sages use this analogy to explain that the original spiritual nature of the soul is now dormant, and it is temporarily replaced with a distorted nature—that of identifying with the body, along with its pains and pleasures. Hinduism teaches that this temporary condition of the soul is the one in which humankind presently finds itself. It also teaches that the original nature of humans, their Sanatana Dharma, only resurfaces when they put themselves in proximity to the spiritual element, either through prayer, worship of images in the temple, through immersion in sacred texts, or by enthusiastically associating with pure devotees of the Lord. Through these methods, say all Hindu texts, the true nature of the soul again rises to the fore, just as the sun eclipses the darkness of night.

To truly understand the Hindu complex of religions, one must grasp the idea of *dharma* in all its richness and subtlety. *Dharma* asks the soul on her sojourn in the material world to look at who she really is, beneath the facade of everyday life. It asks her to penetrate the veil of illusion and to open herself to the spiritual dimensions that lie just beyond her grasp. Hinduism points to a certain nonsectarianism that seeks to unite all religions by looking at their essence, and all people by looking at theirs. This book explores the origins, texts, tenets, practices, rituals, and practitioners of Hinduism, and it hopes to shed some light on Hindu *dharma*.

NOTES

1. The word *Hindu* comes from the Indo-Iranian root *sindhu*, a word that means "river," specifically referring to the Indus River in India. Consequently, the word was originally a geographical marker for anyone living near that particular river. It was first used around 500 B.C.E. The notion of a "Hindu religion," or

"Hindu*ism*," was conceived by Europeans sometime in the nineteenth century, conveniently (if artificially) combining the indigenous religions of India into one neat "ism."

2. The names of the many Hindu religions and their respective gods may be daunting, but it is helpful to remember that Hinduism acknowledges one ultimate spiritual reality, known as Brahman, and that this reality is comparable to the Western idea of God. Hinduism further teaches that all aspects of God, as represented in the religion's many gods and goddesses, are really so many facets of that same one reality, with hierarchical particularities understood only by scholarly experts and experienced practitioners.

3. See David Levinson, *Religion: A Cross-Cultural Dictionary* (New York: Oxford University Press, 1998). See also the 1999 edition of the "Yearbook of American & Canadian Churches," National Council of the Churches of Christ in the United States, as well as "The American Religious Identification Survey," by The Graduate Center of the City University of New York, http://www.gc.cuny.edu/studies/.

4. Two-thirds of the known Hindu world are Vaishnavas, or those Hindus who emphasize Vishnu as the Supreme Godhead. See Gerald Larson, *India's Agony over Religion* (Albany: State University of New York Press, 1995), p. 20, and Agehananda Bharati, *Hindu Views and Ways and the Hindu-Muslim Interface* (New Delhi: Munshiram Manoharlal, 1981). This statistic implies that the Hindu majority worships Vishnu or one of his incarnations as India's preeminent manifestation of divinity. Given that there are some 800 million Hindus in India alone, Vaishnavism is made up of about 550 million people. This being the case, it is reasonable to assume that an exploration of Vaishnavism might unlock, to a certain degree, the mysteries of Hinduism in general. Furthermore, as Hinduism is such a vast subject, with numerous and diverse traditions, it would be prudent to focus on the one that is numerically most significant. Indeed, it would be impossible to focus on them all.

5. This list of Hinduism's 11 essential principles is a revised version of a similar list found in *Hinduism Today*, a modern magazine on contemporary Hinduism. See the original list online: www.himalayanacademy.com/basics/nineb/. Regarding Varnashrama Dharma, the social system mentioned at the end of this list, traditional Indian society is divided into intellectuals and priests (Brahmins), administrators and warriors (Kshatriyas), mercantile people and farmers (Vaishyas), and those who help the rest of society (Shudras). The system also accounts for those on the spiritual path, including celibate students (Brahmacharis), married couples (Grihasthas), those entering retired life (Vanaprasthas), and wandering mendicants (Sannyasis).

6. *Buddhists* refer to the followers of Siddhartha Gautama, the founder of historical Buddhism 2,500 years ago. *Jains* are religious ascetics with much in common with Buddhists, emphasizing *ahimsa,* or "harmlessness," as Buddhists do, but they come in the lineage of Mahavira, a religious reformer who was Siddhartha's contemporary. *Sikhs,* for their part, represent a tradition founded much later by Guru Nanak, sometime in the sixteenth century. This latter tradition merged Hindu and Islamic doctrine, which was appropriate for the people of the time, for Muslim presence in India was by then well established. These three traditions do not trace their theology to the Vedas, Hinduism's earliest sacred texts, and are thus considered Hindu heterodoxies, if Hindu at all. The modern Indian Constitution (article 25.2) classifies all Buddhists, Jains, and Sikhs as "Hindu," although most traditionalist Hindus object to this inclusion, largely because these religions do not honor the Vedas.

TIMELINE

Determining when significant events in Hindu history occurred is difficult. Discrepancies in different sources are often not merely a matter of a few years, or even of a few decades, but rather of centuries. Hindus believe that this disparity in dating is the result of ulterior motives by early Christian missionaries, who were the first to attempt a chronology of Hindu events. It is believed that their speculative efforts were specifically designed to make Hinduism appear like a Christian derivative. Whatever the truth behind the timeline strategies of the initial Indologists, subsequent scholars often uncritically accepted the dates left to them by their predecessors. Only in the last couple of decades have scholars seriously reconsidered these dates in terms of traditional methods and procedures.

To honor both scholarly considerations and the timeline offered by traditionalists (and a new generation of scholars), this chronology lists the standard, academically derived dates but also adds comments where traditionalists (and others) might disagree. In this way, the reader can see how modern scholars view historical events in Hindu history, and yet they will also be privy to the timeline in which practitioners view these same events.

Most of the significant events of Hinduism occurred in a prehistoric period, more than 5,000 years ago. Hindu history is separated into world cycles called *yugas*, and these are, from the earliest to the most current, Satya-yuga (also called Krita-yuga, lasting 1,728,000 years), Treta-yuga

(1,296,000 years), Dvapara-yuga (864,000 years), and Kali-yuga (432,000 years). These ages constantly recur, like seasons. By Hindu reckoning, the world is currently in the last of these ages, Kali-yuga, with more than 5,000 years of it now elapsed. This means that about 427,000 years of Kali loom large in the future. After that, Satya-yuga will begin again, and so on.

Generally, when Hindu scholars look at their history, they begin 3,000 years before the beginning of the current age. Since Kali began roughly 3000 B.C.E., most Hindu history books begin with 6500 B.C.E. That being the case, most of the events described in Hindu scriptures took place millennia earlier.

6500 B.C.E. Verses from the Rig Veda, India's earliest sacred texts, are said to have been compiled. Others say it took final form in 1200–1000 B.C.E. Aryans were already present in India. Some say the Indus Valley Civilization was born during this era, but others say that it came into being from 3000–1500 B.C.E.

5500 B.C.E. Astrological observations later mentioned in the Puranas.

4750 B.C.E. Scholarly dating for Lord Rama's sojourn in the material world, although tradition places him in Treta-yuga, an epoch of world history almost one million years earlier.

3200–2000 B.C.E. Traditionally accepted date of the Indus Valley Civilization, which is also said to have flourished between 2350–1750 B.C.E.

3112 B.C.E. Traditional date for Krishna's earthly existence. Scholars give him a later date.

3237 B.C.E. Krishna leaves the world. Kali Yuga, the final epoch of world history, begins. Traditionalists say that the Vedic literature was put into written form at roughly this time, although scholars refer to a later date, perhaps 1900 B.C.E. A more conservative estimate would be 1200 B.C.E. for the earliest Vedic texts.

2000–1250 B.C.E. Upanishads, Brahmanas and Aranyakas seem to arise at this time. Early versions of *Mahabharata* and *Ramayana* may appear at this time, too, although scholars point out that accretions are found in later editions ranging from 500 B.C.E.–500 C.E.

1900 B.C.E.   Drying up of Sarasvati River, end of Indus-Sarasvati culture, and end of the Vedic age. After this, the center of civilization in ancient India relocates from the Sarasvati to the Ganges, along with possible migration of Vedic peoples out of India.

1500–500 B.C.E.   Major Upanishads and philosophical sutras are composed, along with the systematization of the six schools of Indian philosophy.

1000–500 B.C.E.   Some see this as the age of the Ramayana, the Mahabharata and the Bhagavad-gita.

623–543 B.C.E.   Life of Siddhartha Gautama, the Buddha. Some Indian, Chinese, and Japanese scholars suggest a later date of almost 100 years.

599–527 B.C.E.   Lifetime of Mahavira, often considered the founder of
or 540–468 B.C.E.   Jainism, although he is part of an ancient line of Jain masters.

500 B.C.E.   Panini, a famous linguist, develops Sanskrit grammar; earlier language is called Vedic Sanskrit.

ca. 400 B.C.E.   Megasthenes, a Greek ambassador to India, writes of Krishna as the Supreme Being, making his work among the earliest historical evidences for Krishna worship.

326 B.C.E.   Invasion of India by Alexander the Great.

324 B.C.E.   Maurya Empire founded by Chandragupta.

273 B.C.E.   Reign of Emperor Ashoka, greatest Mauryan leader who eventually converts to Buddhism.

100 B.C.E.   Heliodorus Column in Besnagar, north-central India, bears an inscription mentioning Vasudeva (Krishna) as a divine being, offering pre-Christian archeological evidence for Krishna worship.

64–225   Emergence of the Kushan dynasty in North India and of the Cholas, Cheras and Pandas in the south.

200   Lifetime of a saint named Tiruvalluvar, poet-weaver who lived near present-day Madras, in South India. He was the author of the *Tirukural* ("Holy Couplets"), a now-classic Tamil work on ethics and politics.

300–900   Sacred texts known collectively as the Puranas reach their finished form. Traditionalists claim much earlier dates for this, although all admit that the Puranas have an ancient oral tradition.

350   Imperial Gupta dynasty (320–540) reigns in India, allowing Hindu theistic traditions to flourish. During this Classical Age, as it came to be known, Hindu forms of literature, poetry, art, architecture, and philosophy are established; and religious traditions, such as Vaishnavism and Shaivism, are patronized by those in power.

365   Roughly the era of Kalidasa, the great Sanskrit poet and dramatist, author of Shakuntala and Meghaduta, although some traditionalists believe he flourished just before the Common Era.

400   Although traditionalists claim that the *Laws of Manu* were written several centuries earlier, this is the date accepted by most scholars, and some say it may be some two hundred years later still.

400   Sage known as Vatsyayana is said to have written the Kamasutra, or the famous text on Hindu erotica.

405–11   Chinese explorer Fa-Hien travels through India and reports back to his people on yogis and Hindu mysticism.

ca. 600–900   Twelve Vaishnava saints, collectively known as the Alvars, flourish in South India, writing 4,000 songs and poems (known as the Nalayira Divya Prabandham). Tradition ascribes earlier dates for most of them.

ca. 650   Lifetime of Shaiva saint Tirujnana Sambandar.

788–820   Generally accepted dates of Adi Shankara, the famous monk-philosopher who emphasized that the world is an illusion and that each living being is ultimately no different from God.

1000–1026   Islamic invasion of India by Mahmud of Ghazni, who conquers Mathura, birthplace of Lord Krishna, and establishes a mosque on the exact site.

1017–1137	Life of Ramanuja, the important devotee-saint of Vaishnavism who opposed Shankara's monistic philosophy.
ca. 1130–1200	Life of Nimbarka, a Vaishnava reformer who emphasized Radha, the female absolute, in the worship of Krishna.
ca. 1150	Life of Jayadeva Goswami, author of the *Gita Govinda*, an esoteric poem about the love of Radha and Krishna. Some say that Radha's name and relationship to Krishna first unfolded in this work, although earlier Puranas also unpacked her very special love for the Lord.
1230–1260	Famous Surya temple at Konarak, Orissa, is constructed.
1238–1317	Life of Ananda Tirtha, also known as Madhva. He was the strongest opponent of Shankara, India's premier Impersonalist philosopher, averring that all living beings are substantially distinct from God.
ca. 1252	Lifetime of Meykandar, the Shaiva saint who systematized the pluralistic school of Shaiva Siddhanta, a philosophical counterpart to Vaishnava theism.
1268–1369	Life of Vedanta Deshika, arguably the most intellectual of South India's Vaishnava philosophers.
1270–1350	Life of Namadeva, famous poet-saint of Maharashtra, whose work is in praise of Lord Vithoba (another name for Vishnu).
1272	Italian explorer Marco Polo visits India en route to China.
1275–96	Life of Jnanadeva, Vaishnava saint and founder of the Varkari school of thought. His most famous disciple is Namadeva.
ca. 1300	Flourishing of Bilvamangala Thakura, also known as Lila-Shuka, a South Indian priest who wrote the magnificent Krishna-karnamrita, a beautiful poem in praise of Radha and Krishna's love. His work particularly influenced Bengali poetry and the internal or contemplative conception of love for Krishna that followed him.
1336	Vijayanagara Empire (1336–1565) of South India. Wealthy patrons of Indian art and culture. European visitors are impressed by its wealth and magnitude.

1346–90	Life of Krittivasa, author of the Bengali version of the Ramayana.
ca. 1350	Life of Appaya Dikshita, South Indian philosopher-saint whose writings attempt to reconcile Vaishnavism and Shaivism.
1415	Bengali poet Badu Chandi Das writes Shri-krishna-kir-tana, an anthology of brilliant songs praising Krishna.
1440–1518	Life of Kabir, a nonsectarian religious reformer with both Muslim and Hindu followers.
1458–1463	Life of Sridhara Swami, famed commentator on the Bhagavata Purana (Shrimad Bhagavatam).
1469–1538	Life of Guru Nanak, founder of Sikhism, a heterodox movement seeking to incorporate the essence of Hindu devotion with Muslim sensibilities.
1479–1545	Life of Vallabhacharya, the Vaishnava reformer who worships Krishna in the form of Shri Nathji and emphasizes parental love of God.
1483–1563	Life of Sur Das, the blind bard of Krishna devotion, whose collected poetry has been compiled in the Sur-sagar.
1486–1533	Life of Chaitanya, Bengali founder of Gaudiya Vaishnavism. He emphasized group chanting and dancing in glorification of Krishna. Seen as a combined manifestation of both Radha and Krishna, he preached enthusiastic devotion and intense love as the culmination of the spiritual pursuit.
1489–1564	Life of Rupa Goswami, foremost of the Six Goswamis of Vrindavan, the saintly systematizers of Sri Chaitanya's language of divine love.
1532–1623	Life of Tulasi Das, who wrote the Rama-charita-manasa, a reworking of the Ramayana in Hindi. This is considered among the most significant works on Vaishnava devotion in a regional language.
1556	Emperor Akbar (reign: 1542–1605) becomes ruler of Hindus and Muslims in India; encourages art, culture, and religious tolerance.
1565	Islam takes over Vijayanagara in the south, although Muslim strength is mainly in the north of India.

ca. 1570	Era of Ekanatha, a Vaishnava saint and composer of devotional poetry in the Marathi language.
ca. 1585	Life of Harivamsa, revolutionary Vaishnava reformer and founder of the Radhavallabha school of thought.
1603–1604	Sikh Guru by the name of Arjun compiles the Adi Granth, which becomes the primary Sikh scripture.
1605	Famous Sikh Golden Temple is completed at Amritsar, in the Punjab.
1608–1649	Life of Tukaram, a poet particularly remembered for his *abhangas*, "unbroken hymns," to Krishna. He is considered among the most important of the early Marathi composers.
1613–1614	British East India Company sets up trading post at Surat.
1615–1618	Islamic Mughals grant Britain the right to trade and to establish factories in India.
ca. 1628–88	Life of Kumaraguruparar, beloved poet-saint of the south who established a monastery in Varanasi and popularized Shaiva Siddhanta philosophy.
1658	Muslim leader Aurangzeb (1618–1707) becomes Mughal emperor. His harsh treatment of Hindus contributes, within 100 years, to the dissolution of the Mughal Empire.
1708	Govind Singh, tenth and last of the original Sikh gurus, is assassinated.
1708–1737	Jai Singh II builds astronomical observatories in Delhi, Jaipur, Ujjain, Benares, and Mathura.
1718–1775	Life of Ramprasad Sen, the Bengali Shakta poet whose mellifluous poetry in honor of the Goddess is recited throughout India even today.
ca. 1750	Kamalakanta Bhattacharya, like the poet Sen, glorifies the goddess with beautiful verse and stimulates a rise in devotional Shaktism, particularly in Bengal.
ca. 1750	Era of Baladeva Vidyabhusana, a central organizer of the Gaudiya school of Vedanta. He is famous for his Govinda-bhashya commentary on the Vedanta-sutra, a standard Hindu text.

1764	British defeat the Mughal Emperor of the time and consequently become rulers of Bengal, the then richest province in India
1781–1830	Life of Sahajananda Swami, the Gujarati founder of the Swaminarayan sect (a reform movement in Vaishnavism).
1785	Indologist Charles Wilkins translates the Bhagavad Gita into English for the first time.
1803–1882	Life of Ralph Waldo Emerson, the "transcendentalist" American poet whose interest in the Bhagavad Gita and the Upanishads helped to popularize them in the United States.
1818–1878	Life of Shiva Dayal, founder of the esoteric reformist Radhasoami sect.
1824–1883	Life of Swami Dayananda Sarasvati, founder of the Arya Samaj (1875), a Hindu reform movement focused on the importance of the Vedas, India's sacred texts.
1828	Ram Mohan Roy (1772–1833) founds the Brahmo Samaj in Calcutta. Like the Arya Samaj, this is a Hindu reform movement. But instead of focusing on the Vedas, this movement seeks to bring Hinduism into the modern era by rejecting many of India's traditional teachings and values.
1831–1891	Life of Russian mystic Madame H. P. Blavatsky, founder of the Theosophical Society, which brought aspects of Hindu thought to the West.
1836–1886	Life of Ramakrishna, the Bengali Shakta saint, who not only popularized worship of the Goddess but preached a form of Shakta universalism in which he attempted to incorporate all religious truth.
1838–1914	Life of Vaishnava reformer Bhaktivinoda Thakura, who was born in Biranagara (Ulagrama) in the Nadia district of West Bengal. A learned scholar with intense missionary passion, he spoke Bengali, Sanskrit, English, Latin, Urdu, Persian, and Oriya. His literary works and universalist Vaishnava conception revolutionized Hindu thought in India and penetrated the West as well.

1850	First English translation of the Rig Veda by H. H. Wilson, who was the original holder of Oxford University's Boden Chair of Sanskrit.
1851	Sir M. Monier-Williams (1819–1899) publishes the first English-Sanskrit Dictionary after three decades of research.
1861–1941	Life of Bengali poet Rabindranath Tagore, awarded the Nobel Prize for Literature in 1913.
1863–1902	Life of Swami Vivekananda, Ramakrishna's dynamic missionary to the West and pivotal speaker at the 1893 World Parliament of Religions conference in Chicago.
1869–1948	Life of Mohandas (Mahatma) Gandhi, Indian nationalist and political activist whose central strategy was nonviolent disobedience.
1872–1950	Life of Aurobindo Ghosh, Bengali nationalist and mystic.
1873–1906	Life of Swami Rama Tirtha, whose philosophical focus is "practical Vedanta," that is, trying to bring Hindu thought into modern times.
1874–1937	Life of Srila Bhaktisiddhanta Saraswati Thakura, the son of Bhaktivinoda Thakura and spiritual master of Srila A. C. Bhaktivedanta Swami Prabhupada. Born as Bimala Prasad, he gradually became known as a living encyclopedia, so vast was his learning. At initiation, he was given the name Varshabhanavi-dayita Dasa. Through his many published books and periodicals and through the opening of his 64 temples, he became one of the most important Vaishnava teachers of his time, with numerous disciples throughout India and parts of Europe.
1876–1990	Max Muller, pioneer of Indic studies, publishes a 50-volume tome entitled, "Sacred Books of the East"—English translations of Oriental scriptures.
1877–1947	Life of Ananda Coomaraswamy, renowned interpreter of Indian art and culture to the West.
1879–1966	Life of Sadhu T. L. Vaswani, poet, humanitarian, and founder of several educational Institutions.

1879–1950	Life of Ramana Maharshi, Hindu renunciant, impersonalist philosopher, and mystic of South India.
1887–1963	Life of Swami Shivananda, Hindu universalist and founder of Divine Life Society.
1888–1975	Life of Sarvepalli Radhakrishnan, renaissance philosopher, eminent writer, and independent India's first vice-president and second president.
1893	Swami Vivekananda represents Hinduism at Chicago's Parliament of Religions, the first worldwide interfaith conference, setting the tone for modern Western understanding of the religion.
1893–1952	Life of Paramahamsa Yogananda, mystic Hindu and founder of the Self Realization Fellowship (1925). His now famous *Autobiography of a Yogi* (1946) universalized and demystified India's spiritual traditions for the modern West.
1857–1920	Nationalist leader Bal Bangadhar Tilak demands complete independence from Britain and writes a political commentary on the Bhagavad Gita.
1896–1977	Life of spiritual leader A.C. Bhaktivedanta Swami Pradhupada. He was the founder of the International Society for Krishna Consciousness (ISKCON) and author of numerous translations and commentaries on traditional Vaishnava literature, and his movement still thrives in every corner of the world.
1917–93	Life of Swami Chinmayananda, writer, lecturer, and Hindu renaissance man. He was founder of the Chinmaya Mission and a co-founder of the Vishva Hindu Parishad, spiritual and political organizations, respectively.
1924	Archaeologist Sir John Marshall (1876–1958) discovers relics of the Indus Valley Civilization. He begins large-scale excavations and establishes precedents for modern scholarly understanding of Hindu history.
1925	K.V. Hedgewar (1890–1949) founds Rashtriya Swayamsevak Sangh (RSS), a Hindu nationalist movement with political concerns.

1928	Hindu leader Jawaharlal Nehru drafts plan for a free India and becomes president of the Congress Party in 1929.
1938	Activist K. M. Munshi founds Bharatiya Vidya Bhavan in Bombay to preserve, develop and distribute Indian culture.
1944	A. C. Bhaktivedanta Swami Prabhupada founds *Back to Godhead* magazine, a periodical based on the universal principles of Vaishnava spirituality.
1947	India gains independence from Britain on August 15. As a result, Pakistan arises as a separate Islamic nation.
1948	Mahatma Gandhi is assassinated by a Hindu fanatic named Nathuram Godse, who was responding to Gandhi's concessions to Muslim demands.
1949	India's new constitution, written primarily by B. R. Ambedkar, a renowned political activist, declares that there will no longer be "discrimination" against any citizen because of caste and that "untouchability," as a concept, will be abolished. The constitution makes Hindi the official national language.
1950	India is declared a secular republic. Prime Minister Jawaharlal Nehru determines to modernize the nation.
1951	India's Bharatiya Janata Sangh (BJP), still its most active political party, is founded.
1957	Shivaya Subramuniyaswami founds Himalayan Academy and opens America's first Hindu temple.
1964	Vishva Hindu Parishad (VHP), a prominent Hindu religious nationalist movement, is founded to address India's growing secularism.
1965	A. C. Bhaktivedanta Swami Prabhupada sails West and a year later incorporates his worldwide Vaishnava mission.
1966	Nehru's daughter, Indira Gandhi, becomes Prime Minister of India, following L. B. Shastri, who took office after Nehru's death in 1964.

1967   Height of the Hippie Era ("the Summer of Love"), in which eastern mysticism became a tangible part of pop culture. First Western Ratha-yatra festival, in San Francisco, a celebration originating in Puri, India, in honor of Lord Jagannath (Krishna).

1979   Shivaya Subramuniyaswami founds *Hinduism Today*, an international Hindu newspaper intended to promote Hindu solidarity.

1984   Indira Gandhi is assassinated by her Sikh bodyguards, and her son Rajiv replaces her in office.

1990   ISCOWP (The International Society for Cow Protection) is incorporated in the state of Pennsylvania. It was begun as a nonprofit educational organization. William and Irene Dove (Balabhadra das and Chayadevi dasi), disciples of A.C. Bhaktivedanta Swami Prabhupada, are its managing directors.

1991   Rajiv Gandhi, who succeeded his mother Indira, as Prime Minister of India is also assassinated.

1992   Third Global Forum of Spiritual Leaders for Human Survival meets in Rio de Janeiro in conjunction with the Earth Summit (UNCED). Hindu views of nature, the environment, and traditional values give guidance to the 70,000 delegates attending.

1992   Founding of the *Journal of Vaishnava Studies*, an academic quarterly esteemed by scholars worldwide.

1992   Hindu radicals demolish Babri Masjid, a mosque built at Lord Rama's birth site, adding fuel to already hostile relations between Hindus and Muslims.

1994   Harvard University, in a sustained research project, identifies more than 800 Hindu temples actively functioning in the United States.

1994   Mata Amritanandamayi (1953–), a much loved female saint of Kerala, South India, is named 1993 Hindu of the Year.

1995   Largest Hindu temple in the Western world is opened by Swaminarayan people in England.

1995	Dharam Hinduja Institute of Indic Research (DHIIR) at Cambridge is established through a generous donation from the Hinduja Foundation (UK) in memory of Dharam Hinduja (1969–1992), the son of Mr. S. P. Hinduja, Chairman of the Hinduja Foundation (UK).
1995	World Hindu Conference in South Africa. Organized and addressed by the President, Nelson Mandela himself, the conference was the first of its kind and attracted representatives from 30 countries.
1997	Oxford Centre for Hindu and Vaishnava Studies, OCHS, is founded as an independent academy for the study of Hindu culture, religion, languages, literature, philosophy, history, arts and society, in all periods and in all parts of the world. The Centre, located in Oxford, England, works closely with Oxford University to meet the highest standards of academic integrity, originality and excellence.
1998	Sulekha, an internet service run by and for Indians, is now the largest and most popular online community and social/professional networking mechanism for Hindus in the world.

1

HISTORY OF FOUNDATION

In Hinduism today, there are fundamentally three views of foundation. Two share prominence in the academic community and one represents a long-standing traditionalist account. This chapter briefly looks at all three.

To begin, scholarly ideas about the early development of Hinduism are in a state of flux. The classical academic theory centers on the Indus Valley civilization said to have flourished from 3000 to 1800 B.C.E.[1] Completely unknown until its rediscovery in the 1920s, it shares a unique position with Mesopotamia, China, and Egypt as one of the four earliest civilizations known to humans. In its heyday, the Indus Valley was surprisingly advanced, with planned cities, agriculture, writing, architecture, and so on. Her first excavated sites were on the Indus River, in the northwest of the Indian subcontinent, which explains how the project received its name. It is also called the Harappan civilization, after one of the cities unearthed in the region.[2] At its height, which scholars say was 2200 B.C.E., the Indus civilization boasted an area that was larger than Europe.

A century after this civilization waned (circa 1500 B.C.E.), or so the theory goes, a nomadic Indo-European tribe migrated into northern India from the steppes of Russia and/or Central Asia. This is called the Aryan Invasion theory, for the migrants are said to have come from Aryan stock.[3] "Aryan," of course, is a word that is familiar in the modern West. However, the word was not originally associated with the blond-haired, blue-eyed ideal of Nazi Germany, even if, the contemporary world, it is often hard to think otherwise.[4] Originally, the word comes from the Sanskrit root *arya*, which means "noble." Historically, Aryans can be traced to the Indo-Iranians, who inhabited parts of what are now Iran, Afghanistan, and India. The basic root *arya* is found in the words "Iran" (the original name for Persia) and even "Ireland."[5] It is also found in early Sanskrit texts, where the exact same word refers to the higher echelon of ancient Indian society. In English, the word *aryan* is related to "aristocratic," which is close to a literal translation.

These original Aryans, upon entering India, are said to have brought with them the Vedic literature, now respected as India's earliest and most sacred texts, and the religious tradition at the base of this literature. Combining this foreign culture with the indigenous beliefs of the native Indians, Hinduism gradually grew into the conglomerate of religions found in India today.

This theory was initially propounded by Christian scholars, who came to India with preconceptions based on the Bible. These were men and women who favored literalism in scriptural understanding and, based on interpretations of the day, viewed the creation of the world as occurring in roughly 4000 B.C.E. This date, in fact, was at the forefront of their minds when hypothesizing the time periods associated with the Indus Valley, the Aryan Migration theory, and the Vedas, the archaic texts of the Hindus. Thus, they rejected the Hindu view that the indigenous culture of India went back tens of thousands of years and put forward, instead, their now classical theory of Hindu origins. This highly motivated classical theory is now being reevaluated by archeologists and religious historians, some of whom see it as terribly outmoded.[6]

INDIGENOUS ARYANS

The new, emerging theory, which constitutes the second scholarly theory under discussion, is that the Aryan invasion quite possibly never happened. Based on new methods in archeology, cultural study, astronomical investigations, and literary analysis, findings are now suggesting that Indian civilization is much older than scholars thought.[7] The Vedas, as a result, are older as well. Most important, perhaps, findings now show that all early aspects of Indian culture were most likely produced internally, with no invasion or migration, but, rather, just by indigenous peoples in what has come to be called "the cradle of civilization."

Although doubts about the Indo-Aryan invasion were initially expressed by Indian scholars, mainstream Western academics have entered the fray.[8] A significant number of archaeologists, both Indian and Western, have now admitted that there is no concrete evidence to support the theory of external Indo-Aryan origins. In addition, the philological and linguistic evidence that had originally been used to support the theory of outside invasions has been called into question and reinterpreted. Thus, many scholars are now inclined to believe that the Indo-Aryans and their culture might have been indigenous to the subcontinent all along, and that the Indus civilization itself might have indeed been Vedic, without outside influence. At present, the scholarly world is still divided on the subject, exploring the evidence from various points of view.[9] At one time, however, the Aryan Invasion theory was accepted as fact, and most textbooks on Hinduism, until about 1985, clearly reflect this.

HINDU ORIGINS

Now that we have explored the two prevailing academic theories, we next examine the theory of Hindu origins accepted by the tradition itself.

This latter theory reflects paranormal and metaphysical views of reality, focusing, as it does, on Brahma, a four-headed living entity at the dawn of creation.[10] This unique entity, state most Hindu texts, created the material world and, along with it, the initial schools of knowledge that eventually blossomed into contemporary Hinduism. The Brahma story is significant because it represents the most widely held view of foundations articulated by Hindus today.

Hindu creation stories abound, but the most popular are found in the Bhagavata Purana, the cream of ancient India's wisdom texts, especially in its First through Third books. Here we read that before time and space, there was only Vishnu, the Supreme Lord. He alone existed, floating in celestial sleep—in a type of yoga, or mystical trance—on a vast ocean of primordial elements. With each breath, multiple bubble-like universes emanated from his body, waiting to be brought to life.

As each of these countless universes floated away from him, he, by his mystic potency, entered into each of them. Now, in his expanded form in each universe, he lay down on the coils of a thousand-hooded serpent, who gently rocked him back and forth, anticipating the momentous act of creation. As Vishnu himself, still in mystic slumber, contemplated this pivotal act, a magnificent golden lotus sprouted from his navel. The lotus shot up, through infinity, blossoming into a thousand-petal whorl. Sitting at the very top was Brahma, the first being of creation, in full adulthood.

Wherever Brahma looked, he saw only darkness. Sun, moon, and firmament were not yet created, and no one inhabited the rudimentary worlds around him. In desperation, he looked to his right, and then to his left and

Vishnu, the Supreme God, source of Brahma, the creator of the universe. © 2003 Mandala Publishing, www.mandala.org.

in front and behind. The intensity of his search made four heads appear, to see in each of the four directions. Even with this advantage, he could see nothing, nor could he understand who he was, or his purpose for being.

Anxious for answers, Brahma climbed down the lotus stem, and, as he moved downward, he observed a whirlpool of unformed planets, budding elements, and incomplete solar systems. He started to feel an impulse that perhaps he was supposed to help complete the masterpiece that he saw unfinished all around him, but he had no idea how to approach this ambitious task. Bewildered, he turned and began his journey back up the lotus stem.

And then he heard it: "Ta-pa." Two syllables. Listening intently, he heard them again—"Ta-pa"—and he intuited their meaning. The Sanskrit word *tapas* means "penance" or "austerity." As Brahma understood it, Lord Vishnu was telling him to perform penance and austerity, and that only by doing so would he realize who he was and what he was meant to do. And so with unbridled enthusiasm, now again situated atop his lotus cradle, he performed the austerity of entering into deep meditation for 1,000 celestial years.

Finally, his meditations bore fruit. As he awakened from a trance, the illusion that separates matter from spirit dissolved, and he saw the spiritual realm in all its glory. Overwhelmed by the Lord Vishnu's original form, by his wonderful associates and transcendental environment, Brahma composed hundreds of poetic verses, which were later compiled in a book known as the Brahma-samhita. With this vision, he had attained enlightenment, which gave him knowledge of who he truly was, as the creator assistant of Vishnu, and exactly what he was meant to do—and he now knew *how* to do it as well. Then, regaining composure, he turned his attention to the mission at hand. From his powerful mind issued forth progeny and from them an impressive array of species to fill the planets, the waters, and skies; the lotus stem now housed 14 divisions of planetary system, with many universes and descendents of Brahma.

Of all Brahma's initial sons, Narada was most dear and perhaps most important in our present context. Brahma had explained to him the truth of the spiritual realm and asked him to share this with the multitudes who now populated the various material universes. Ages passed and Narada's mission knew its greatest success when, in more recent times, say, 5,000 years ago, he conveyed the message to Vyasa, the renowned compiler of the Vedic literature, India's ancient wisdom texts.

Vyasa took the one original Veda and divided it into four, and these he edited for ease of understanding. He further compiled the Mahabharata and the Puranas, ancient Hindu scriptures collectively known as "the Fifth Veda." Each of these he entrusted to scholars of irreproachable character, and they in turn taught the texts to their disciples and grand-disciples. Thus the respective schools of Vedic thought were established. These schools, says the tradition, eventually gave rise to the Hinduism of today.

It is still in the esoteric lineages that the essential core of Vedic truth is passed down: Brahma to Narada to Vyasa to contemporary teachers. This initial lineage is known as the Brahma Sampradaya. Shiva, the demigod in charge of universal destruction, is also the founder of an early lineage, known as the Rudra Sampradaya. Lakshmi, the Goddess of Fortune, wife of Vishnu, founded another. And the Four Kumaras, saintly personalities from a time in the distant past, began yet another. These four lines of disciplic descent were systematized by Madhvacharya, Vishnu Swami, Ramanuja, and Nimbarka, respectively, the best of the great teacher-saints from medieval India. There are other traditional lineages, too, but these are not mentioned in the Bhagavata Purana.[11] All such lineages teach that serious spiritual aspirants should live their lives in such a way that truth naturally opens up, like Brahma's lotus in the beginning of creation.

In fact, commentators on the Bhagavata Purana explain that the Brahma story, in addition to revealing something about cosmic creation, is a metaphor for humans' spiritual sojourn. Like Brahma, humans are connected to their past through an umbilical cord—the lotus stem of their genetic background. In addition, humans are born in ignorance, comparable to the darkness of Brahma's yet uncreated worlds. Like him, humans must determinedly question their identity and purpose. And when they hear the call of the Lord, they must be willing to deeply contemplate their reason for being and to perform austerities—to do whatever it takes—to reach the goal.

The creation story as explained here is typical in India, with countless variations depending on exactly which scripture one reads. It is perhaps less typical to hear that Brahma not only created the world but also the first lineage of transcendental knowledge, that is, Sanatana Dharma, the Brahma Sampradaya, in which he revealed truths that he directly received from God. Yet this idea of Hindu origins is implicit in the Bhagavata Purana, which further says that what Brahma heard from Vishnu stands at the threshold of modern Hindu thought, with seeds of ideas that eventually blossomed into contemporary Hindu practice, regardless of the specific modern-day tradition. Although this unveiling of Hindu origins is indeed supernatural, it gives Hindus a sense of where their tradition originates.

THE ORIGINAL VEDAS

No account of Hindu foundations would be complete without a brief look at the Vedas, the original scriptures at the root of modern Hinduism. Unlike the great Hindu epics (the Ramayana and the Mahabharata) and the Puranas (the many histories that contain life stories of saints and Incarnations of God), these are not scriptures that are commonly used today, and most Hindus do not know their contents. The Vedas are, rather, antecedents to the modern Hindu tradition, and all subsequent scriptures and philosophical outlooks necessarily defer to them.[12]

The four Vedas are the original Vedic scriptures, comprising four books known as Rig, Sama, Yajur, and Atharva Vedas. These texts were originally transmitted orally. The miracle of how these texts were "passed down" has been noted by numerous scholars. Like the Masoretic versions of the Hebrew Bible, the Vedas were "accented," or preserved by elaborate mnemonic devices meant to ensure their longevity. In addition, it was taught that harsh reactions from "on high" awaited those who changed or mutilated the text in any way. As a result, the Vedas have been transmitted over several millennia with impeccable fidelity, complete with accent and pronunciation.

Although the exact sounds were retained, however, most scholars question whether the original meanings were retained as well. Also, the Vedic literature is believed to have been many times its current length, and that most Vedic texts are no longer extant. Hindu priests today generally believe that what currently exists is representative of the overall corpus, but no one really knows.

The name *Rig*, which is the first of the four Vedas, comes from a Sanskrit word that means "ritual," and, accordingly, this Veda contains 1,017 hymns and prayers that were meant to be used in sacred rituals. These were rituals specifically constructed to appease the countless gods of the Vedic pantheon, which the Rig Veda, specifically, narrowed down to 33. Each god represented atmospheric, terrestrial, or celestial concerns. Their names should be known: Indra (god of war and weather), Surya (god of the sun), Agni (god of fire), and Varuna (guardian of the cosmic order and moral law), among others.[13]

The gods of the Rig Veda are often personifications of nature or of higher universal powers. In this way, India's visionary sages hoped to promote communion with a *spiritualized* world, that is, communion with ordinary phenomenon from a nonmaterial point of view. Ultimately, the sages were clear that the many gods of the Rig Veda are actually one; they were various representations of the same divine essence, the Oversoul of the universe. The harmony between "the one and the many" is central to Vedic religion. Unity in diversity; that is, all the gods are actually various manifestations of the same one absolute truth, and yet they are different as well. This idea filtered down into later Hinduism.

The Sama Veda, which is the second of the four Vedas, consists of various portions of the Rig and some other hymns as well, but now all of these prayers were put to melody. *Sama* means "singing," and this Veda's almost 1,600 verses include strict rules on how to chant or sing the ritualistic songs meant to appease the gods. The Yajur Veda is the "Veda of Rituals," containing almost 2,000 verses in 40 chapters. Many of these verses, too, are repeated from the Rig Veda, and they are constructed in such a way as to be used in similar rituals.

The word *Atharva*, which is the name of the fourth and final of the original Vedas, refers to a priest who knows the secret lore of the ancients. Thus, this Veda of some 6,000 verses is filled with incantations and invocations from antiquity. It differs from the other three in that it elaborates on material sciences, like Ayurveda (a holistic system of medicine) and also on odd-seeming spells for manipulating material nature. It includes rules for oblations and sacrifices, prayers for averting evil people and for overcoming diseased conditions. This Veda even has incantations for the destruction of foes, for fulfilling personal desires, and so on, mostly for people's material needs.

Attached to each of the Vedas are books called Brahmanas and Aranyakas, which consist of commentarial traditions for priests and forest dwellers, respectively.

Included in the original Vedic corpus is the Upanishads, a collection of 108 philosophical dissertations. Unlike the four original Vedas, these are highly technical expositions on the nature of ultimate reality, using logic and reason. The Upanishads mainly focus on establishing the absolute as nonmaterial, calling it Brahman, the eternal, nonmanifest reality, the source and ultimate shelter of all that is. This Brahman is said to be incomprehensible because it is without qualities or form. The Vaishnava sages of India, however, suggest that Brahman is best understood as having no *material* qualities and form; qualities and forms that are inherently *spiritual*, say the sages, is a different matter altogether. The Upanishads constitute the beginning of Hindu philosophy as it is known today.

What is important to know about the Vedas—particularly the four original Vedas—is that although they are still considered the ultimate authority in Hindu religion, they deal mainly with life in the material world. As opposed to theistic traditions such as Vaishnavism (the worship of Vishnu), the Vedas are more concerned with harmony and happiness in the world of three dimensions, and for graduation to the heavenly planets. Vaishnavism, on the other hand, seeks to take practitioners beyond liberation, beyond the heavenly planets, to the platform of love of God. In other words, Vaishnavism's goal is not simply acclimation to the world of here and now but also to establish the living being in his or her original position, as a lover of God in the spiritual realm.

Vedic rituals, moreover, are now severely outdated. They involved elaborate sacrificial offerings—often animal offerings—complete with highly trained ritual priests and ornate fire coliseums. These complex ritualistic performances have long ceased to be vital, and the old Vedic hymns are no longer pertinent in the same way, although some of the procedures and prayers are still used by priests today. They exist now primarily as acts and words of empowerment, based on "revelation" (*shruti*), as Vedic texts were originally known, not human-made but given by God. Today, the remnants of Vedic ideas and agendum are merely incorporated into newer rites. The only part of the Vedas that continues to have more than mere referential

Madan Mohan Temple, the ancient remains of an important Vaishnava shrine, found in the sacred area of Braj, Uttar Pradesh, North India. Courtesy of the author.

meaning is the Upanishads, for the underlying philosophy of these texts is still functional in terms of later Hindu tradition. It is these Upanishads, in fact, that form the basis of the "Fifth Veda"—the epics and the Puranas, or the ancient histories—which are the Hindu texts most used today, serving to define the modern Hindu tradition.

NOTES

1. In 2002, the new epithet "Sindhu Sarasvati Civilization" was introduced into Indian schoolbooks. This has become the new designation for what was previously known as the Indus Valley civilization. The Sanskritized *sindhu* instead of the Western *indus* and the addition of "Saraswati," an ancient river central to Hinduism's sacred geography, is meant to suggest that the Indus Valley civilization was originally part of Vedic or indigenous Indian culture. This is an attempt by traditionalists to deny the validity of the Aryan Invasion theory.

2. Harappa is a city in the Punjab, northeast Pakistan, just adjacent to where the Ravi River used to flow. The modern town is built beside the remains of Harappa proper, indicating a fortified city from ancient times, a now legendary city that was part of Cemetery H and the Indus Valley civilization. It is said that it existed from 3300 B.C.E. to 1600 B.C.E.

Another city, Mohenjo-daro, is often mentioned in conjunction with Harappa, although the two are 400 miles away from each other. This one is located in the Sindh province of Pakistan. As in Harappa, much archaeological evidence for the Indus Valley civilization has been discovered here, even if the implications and significance of this evidence are questionable.

3. *Aryan* refers to the ancestors of the Indo-European family of nations. They likely lived in Bactria, that is, between the Oxus River and the Hindukush Mountains. The Aryan family of languages includes Persian and Sanskrit, as well as all European tongues except Basque, Turkish, Hungarian, and Finnish. According to scholarly theory, before the Aryans entered the Indian subcontinent (ca 1500 B.C.E.), they were in close contact with the ancestors of the Iranians, as can be inferred by similarities between Sanskrit and the earliest surviving Iranian dialect.

4. There is an interesting series of events that led to the German appropriation of the term *aryan*. Briefly, German philologists from early in the twentieth century argued that the original Aryans came from Germany or perhaps Scandinavia. The Vedic Aryans, according to this theory, were ethnically related to the Goths, Vandals, and other ancient Germanic peoples of the Völkerwanderung. After leaving the area and, centuries later, exacting a triumphant return, the Germans naturally "reclaimed" their Aryan birthright.

5. Connections between early Persian religion and the birth of Hinduism need to be further explored. The hymns of the Rig Veda, earliest of Hindu texts, and the Gathas, the Persian literature, show a fundamental similarity in grammar, vocabulary, and even in the names of deities and underlying theology. It is thus clear that they derive from a common parent language and perhaps even a common cultural heritage.

6. The most comprehensive and up-to-date work in this area is found in Edwin Bryant, *The Quest for the Origins of Vedic Culture: The Indo-Aryan Migration Debate* (New York: Oxford University Press, 2001). See also Bryant's volume co-edited with Laurie L. Patton, *Indo-Aryan Controversy: Evidence and Inference in Indian History* (Richmond: Curzon, 2005).

7. Klaus Klostermaier represents the contingent of scholars who push the Vedic date back by several thousand years. It is not that he merely accepts traditionalist views, but he bases his findings on modern research. For more, see his book *Hinduism: A Short History* (New York: Oneworld Publications, 2000), pp. 9, 36, 42. It is generally understood that the dating of all early Hindu literature is tentative. This is particularly true for the four traditional Vedas, because here we are confronted with material that was transmitted orally in archaic Sanskrit for centuries before its compilation. See also Arvind Sharma's article, "Method in the Study of Hinduism," in his edited volume, *The Study of Hinduism* (Columbia, SC: University of South Carolina Press, 2003), p. 57.

8. For a good overview of the debate, see Klaus Klostermaier, "Questioning the Aryan Invasion Theory and Revising Ancient Indian History" in *ISKCON Communications Journal*, 6.1, June 1998, as well as Edwin Bryant's response to Klostermaier's article in the subsequent issue (6.2, December 1998). See also the two most widely used Hindu textbooks today: Klaus Klostermaier, *A Survey of Hinduism* (Albany: State University of New York Press, 1994, reprint) and Gavin Flood, *An Introduction to Hinduism* (Cambridge, UK: Cambridge University Press, 1996). Here we find that Klostermaier categorically rejects the Aryan Invasion theory (pp. 35–36), indicating that its premises have been systematically dismantled. Yet Flood leans more toward an acceptance of the theory, at least in modified form (pp. 31–35). He suggests that it was perhaps a gradual "migration" as opposed to an "invasion," although he admits that the matter is far from settled.

9. Again, the various positions held by modern scholars are found in Edwin Bryant, *The Quest for the Origins of Vedic Culture: The Indo-Aryan Migration Debate.*

10. Hinduism recognizes four extremely similar words, all variations on "Brahman." For the purposes of this book, these words are spelled and explained as follows: (1) *Brahman,* the overarching soul of the universe, or God in his most abstract feature; (2) *Brahmin,* the social order composed of intellectuals and priests; (3) *Brahma,* the first created being, existing on the topmost planet in the material universe; Vishnu's chief assistant in creation of the universe; (4) *Brahmanas,* a category of literature associated with the ancient Vedic texts.

11. The other famous lineage in India is the Shankara Sampradaya, which is also traced to Vishnu, the Lord of the Vaishnavas. That the Shankara Sampradaya originates with Vishnu is significant, because Shankarites and Vaishnavas, devotees of Vishnu, differ on several important points of theology and practice and because, in contemporary times, most Shankarites are worshippers of Shiva, the demigod of destruction. Be that as it may, Shankara (ca 788–820 C.E.), the systematizer of this lineage, acknowledged that his spiritual and philosophical heritage comes from a succession of teachers, beginning with Vishnu himself. These teachers are enumerated in a hymn, known as the Parampara-stotra, which is recited by Shankarites to this day, and Vishnu is still acknowledged, in this very hymn, as the originator of the lineage.

12. So much is this the case that, in addition to Sanatana Dharma, most Hindus today refer to their religion as Vaidika Dharma, or "the Vedic Law." Brian K. Smith, an important scholar of Hindu studies, has eloquently stated: "The great paradox of Hinduism ... is that although the religion is inextricably tied to the legitimizing authority of the Veda, in post-Vedic times the subject matter of the Veda was and is largely unknown by those who define themselves

in relation to it. Its contents (almost entirely concerning the meaning and performance of sacrificial rituals that Hindus do not perform) are at best reworked (being, for example, reconstituted into ritual formulas or mantras for use in Hindu ceremonies), and [in] many cases appear to be totally irrelevant for Hindu doctrine and practice." See his book, *Reflections on Resemblance, Ritual, and Religion* (New York: Oxford University Press, 1989), p. 20.

13. According to the Vaishnava tradition, Vishnu "loaned" his names to the various gods, implying that, originally, these names (and the truths at their base) belonged to him. *Shiva*, for example, means "auspicious," and no one is more auspicious than Vishnu. In this way, Vishnu is seen as the ultimate reality behind the many gods of the Vedas. Along similar lines, though Vishnu is himself referred to only rarely in the original Vedic texts, He is described as "all-pervading," encompassing the "three" aspects of space and time—the terrestrial, the celestial, and the atmospheric. Thus, because the gods represent these three as well, as stated in the Vedas, Vishnu is seen as engulfing them all, as embodying their very essence.

2

TEXTS AND MAJOR TENETS

Only the foundational texts of India, the Vedas, along with their attendant Brahmana, Aranyaka, and Upanishadic literature are considered direct revelation from God, as mentioned in Chapter 1. The original four books—the Rig Veda, the Sama Veda, the Yajur Veda, and the Atharva Veda—are basically a series of prayers to the divine, incorporating complex rituals and elaborate fire sacrifices that are the stuff of legend. Here, in this earliest stratum of Indic literature, divinity appears in the form of terrestrial, celestial, and atmospheric deities, individual representations of the Supreme Spirit for specific sacrificial purposes. Many of these sacrifices are replicated today, although in a much abbreviated form and only during special ceremonies. The archaic texts known as the Vedas have largely been replaced by a corpus of secondary literature, and these make up the texts of modern Hinduism.

The vast array of secondary literature, which is also considered sacred, includes the Mahabharata (with its subsection, the Bhagavad Gita, known as the New Testament of India), the Ramayana, and the 18 Puranas, or books of ancient Indian history.[1] Although not revelation as such, these secondary works are considered *revelatory*, providing the Hindu community with the insights of their sages. Thus, for many, these texts are equal in importance to the original Vedas, and, indeed, have come to be known as "the Fifth Veda."

In fact, from a particular point of view, this subsequent literature is considered even *more* important because it is seen as "the Veda for Everyone." Its profound truths are easily accessible and open to all.[2] In these sacred texts one finds the underlying principles that vitalized Vedic rituals in days of old and the functional components that make similar rituals relevant even today. Ironically, then, this secondary literature constitutes the primary texts of modern-day Hinduism.

THE UPANISHADS

The Upanishads are 108 separate texts appended to the Vedas and described as their philosophical elaboration. These works are considered part of the Vedas proper. Despite the many Upanishadic texts known to tradition, only about 13 are currently popular or commonly referred to. In these works one finds a bridge, of sorts, from the vast impersonalism of the Vedas to the religions we now identify as Hinduism. Indeed, even though specific deities are mentioned in the earliest of Vedic texts, the overall tenor of its spiritual message lacks the personalistic theism of later Hindu tradition.

Scholars place the Upanishads at about 700 B.C.E., but tradition pushes it back considerably further. The author of these works is believed to be Vyasa, the compiler of the original Vedas, although most practitioners are willing to admit that he must have had disciples and assorted other helpers in the mammoth task of committing all of this to writing.

The word *upanishad* means "to come and sit down near me," indicating that the texts are properly understood by sitting at the feet of a teacher (*guru*) and learning submissively. All Upanishads focus on the truths underlying Vedic knowledge—the vast reality at the heart of all ritual and sacrifice, the core of spiritual wisdom. Important aphorisms associated with the Upanishads are "You are That" (i.e., Brahman) and "I am Brahman." Naturally, those with a monistic leaning have interpreted these aphorisms as indicating oneness with God. The theistic traditions, however, have explained them in different ways. The Sanskrit texts allow for that. For example, "You are That" can simply mean "you are spirit," which does not necessarily indicate identity with God. Similarly, "I am Brahman" can be understood in a similar way. Indeed, Vaishnavas, or devotees of Vishnu, go through great pains to distinguish between Brahman and "Para"-Brahman, or spirit and the "Supreme" spirit.

The Upanishads themselves make a distinction between impersonalistic understandings of the Absolute and those that are personal, often favoring the latter. For example, the Ishopanishad, Mantra Twelve, offers an admonition against depersonalized conceptions of God: "Those who are engaged in the worship of the gods enter into the darkest region of ignorance and still more so do the worshipers of the impersonal Absolute." Vaishnava commentators say that impersonalists tend to fall into hellish consciousness because they deny God's ability to have personal features, implying that even they have something that God does not. All of our greatest pleasures come from sensual experience, say the Vaishnavas, and God is not to be denied such pleasures. He can see, hear, speak, and love. In short, He can experience things as we do, but without the imperfections associated with a temporary and limited nature.

The Ishopanishad further informs us that God's impersonal feature is essentially an overwhelming white light, purely spiritual, and fully engulfing all who come in its path. It is composed of His personal bodily effulgence, which can be blinding, denying its viewers access to the personal form at its base. In Mantra Fifteen of this same Upanishadic text, the personified Vedas pray, "O my Lord, sustainer of all that lives, Your real face is covered by Your orb of gold. Kindly remove that covering and exhibit Yourself to me, for I adore the Truth." Vaishnava exegesis holds that the mysterious "orb of gold" is the Lord's "impersonal effulgence." In Mantra Sixteen, we further read, "O my Lord, O primeval philosopher, maintainer of the universe, O regulating principle, destination of pure souls, well-wisher of the progenitors of mankind, please remove the effulgence of Your transcendental rays so that I can see Your form of bliss. You are the eternal divine entity, and You are like the sun." For Vaishnavas, then, the impersonal aspect of the Lord is, in a sense, His less substantial side. This is so not only because it is bereft of personal characteristics—characteristics that allow one to have an intimate relationship with God—but because it can actually interfere with the ability to relate to God's form.

To be fair, most Upanishadic texts seem to indicate otherwise. They seem to endorse a more impersonal understanding of the Absolute. But under the guidance of Hinduism's theistic philosophers—who make up the overwhelming majority, whether of Vaishnava, Shaiva, or Shakta leanings—one can understand an entirely intimate and personalistic view of these same texts.

THE MAHABHARATA: THE LONGEST POEM IN WORLD LITERATURE

The Mahabharata comprises some 110,000 Sanskrit couplets—seven times the length of the *Iliad* and the *Odyssey* combined or nearly three times the size of the Judeo-Christian Bible. As an epic of immense proportions, both in terms of length and content, it has become the basis of Indian myth, religion, and philosophical thought. It is within the pages of the Mahabharata (1.57.74), in fact, that we first read of a work that sees itself on the level of the Vedas; it proclaims itself "the Fifth Veda."[3]

According to tradition, the Mahabharata was compiled some 5,000 years ago by the legendary Vyasa, who is seen as the "literary incarnation" of God, meaning that he was empowered specifically for this task. After editing the original Vedas, he wanted to break down its basic truths in a way that the mass of people might understand. Hence, he wrote the Mahabharata, a mammoth work that, as it is said, includes just about everything. As the text itself opines: "If it is not found within these pages, it does not exist."[4]

The Mahabharata contains a wealth of information about ancient Indian society and, more generally, about what motivates people, both good and bad. It offers insights on love, hate, altruism, anger, suffering, and liberation. It teaches the importance of doing one's duty, of honor, integrity, harmlessness, and nonaggression; it explains the futility of war and of its occasional necessity; it stresses how social roles commingle with transcendent ones and how the spiritual pursuit is the zenith of all action.

The substance of the basic story, however, revolves around the furious quarrel between the Pandavas and the Kauravas, two groups of cousins who were nurtured from their earliest years in the chivalrous Kshatriya caste[5]—meaning that they were trained as warriors, administrators, and protectors of the innocent. The quarrel between these two groups escalated into a full-scale civil war, involving gods, yogis (higher beings with magical powers), sages, and royalty. Tradition holds that this war actually occurred—although certain commentators, such as Mahatma Gandhi, Indian politician and pacifist, see it more as a metaphor—and that it happened during the time of Vyasa 5,000 years ago. In the midst of it all, the character looming largest is Krishna, the Supreme Being—Vishnu in a more human-like form. The Mahabharata depicts him as a friend of the Pandavas, charioteer and confidante to the central protagonist, a Pandava leader whose name was Prince Arjuna.[6]

THE BHAGAVAD GITA: THE NEW TESTAMENT OF INDIA

Although widely published as a book unto itself, the Bhagavad Gita originally appeared as an episode in the Sixth Section of the Mahabharata. It consists of 700 verses in 18 chapters and is often referred to as the Gitopanishad. In other words, it follows the literary style and philosophical conclusions of the earlier Upanishads, the esoteric books of knowledge appended to the Vedas.

Gita means "song," and bhagavad refers to "God, the possessor (*vat*) of all opulence (*bhaga*)." The Bhagavad Gita, therefore, is "The Song of the All-Opulent One," embodying the essential teachings of Lord Krishna.

On the eve of the great Mahabharata battle, with multiple armies arrayed on the battlefield at Kurukshetra, not far from Delhi in present-day India, Krishna spoke the Bhagavad Gita, the philosophical poem that, according to some, is the most important portion of the larger epic.

The text comes to us in the form of a dialogue: Prince Arjuna, putting aside his duty as an administrative officer, decides not to fight, although he is standing right there on the battlefield, and the battle is about to begin. His decision to desist will affect the lives of huge numbers. It is motivated by pragmatic if also emotional concerns: his kinsmen and teachers are in the opposing army. These particular family members, although noble and virtuous in numerous ways, have broken the law, and it is Arjuna's duty to bring them to justice.

Krishna, the Supreme Personality of God-head, acts as charioteer for his friend and devotee prince Arjuna. © 1998 Mandala Publishing, www.mandala.org.

Krishna, who has agreed to become the driver of Arjuna's chariot, is witness to Arjuna's reservation. He watches as the noble Prince turns from courageous warrior to a man with second thoughts. Arjuna's face reveals his ever-deepening realization that he must kill relatives and friends, and he begins to question the entire militaristic enterprise that lay before him. Feeling compassion, Krishna eloquently reminds Arjuna of his immediate social duty as a warrior on whom people are depending, and, more important, of his religious duty as an eternal spiritual entity in relationship with God. Surprisingly, Krishna does not tell Arjuna to avoid the war and to adopt the life of a renounced spiritualist. Rather, he tells him to do his duty on the battlefield—that, in the long run, the battle would be the lesser of two evils. The relevance and universality of Krishna's teachings transcend the immediate historical setting of Arjuna's battlefield dilemma.

The dialogue moves through a series of questions and answers that brings Arjuna, along with subsequent readers, to an understanding of certain fundamental metaphysical concepts. These include the distinction between the body and the soul, or between matter and spirit; the logic of reincarnation; the principle of nonattached action, or how to work dispassionately and for a higher purpose; the virtues and mechanics of various forms of discipline and meditation (*yoga*); and the place of knowledge (*gyana*) and devotion (*bhakti*) in pursuit of the spirit. Krishna explains the modes of nature—goodness, passion, and ignorance—and how these qualities impact on peoples' lives. He also explains the nature of God and the purpose of existence. Ultimately, Krishna teaches Arjuna that perfection lies not in renunciation of the world, but rather in disciplined action, performed without attachment to results. He urges Arjuna to fight, but with a sense of love and spiritual purpose.

In India, at the time, the Bhagavad Gita was revolutionary. The prevailing idea of spirituality had always been one of renunciation, of leaving the world behind to practice asceticism and contemplation in solitude. This, in fact, was Arjuna's leaning: When the question of battle became particularly poignant for him, he opted for retreating, for taking shelter of a more peaceful religiosity. Appealing though this option might have seemed, Krishna pointed out to him that it would, in fact, cause more harm than good. After all, the lives of many would be on his head, and, clearly, his decision to renounce was made hastily, with self-interested motives. This is why the Bhagavad Gita is considered the New Testament of India: Krishna gave a new dispensation, a new approach to spiritual perfection, and he deemed it superior to the traditional "inactive" model. Rather, he taught Arjuna that action is superior to inaction, but only when it is done for the right purposes, that is, when it is done for him, for God.

THE RAMAYANA: THE WORLD'S GREATEST LOVE STORY

The other great Sanskrit epic, the Ramayana—"the story of Rama," also an incarnation of Vishnu, the Oversoul of the Universe—is about 24,000 verses, which makes it roughly a quarter the length of the Mahabharata. It is said to originate in a previous age, about 2 million years ago, although scholars, naturally, give it a much later date. The sage Valmiki was the first to present it in written form, but it is a story that existed long before he committed it to writing. There are many retellings that came after Valmiki's version as well, and, in fact, most Hindus know these other, regional versions, for they appear in vernacular languages, whereas Valmiki's is in Sanskrit, an archaic tongue known mainly by the intellectual elite.

The Ramayana is often relished for its sheer beauty: As examples, one need look no further than its Sanskrit poetry, its provocative setting, and its profound dialogue. The beauty is also evident in the sense of morals and ethics found in its pages, in the ideals it encourages in its readers, and in the wide canopy of emotions it brings to the fore. Most of all, the inspirational personalities depicted in its pages are the highest peaks in the Ramayana's overwhelming beauty.

First, there is Lord Rama himself. Clearly described as "God on earth" (*avatar*), Rama is tall, strong, and righteous. His beautiful features are surpassed only by his inner beauty. He is the embodiment of virtue, a true hero, who often shows his more "human" side, making him a particularly endearing manifestation of God. He loves others and feels pain, especially when the woman so close to his heart, Sita, is taken away from him. She is kidnapped by the evil Ravana, Rama's archenemy in the Ramayana, and Rama must get her back. How he does so, with integrity and with the help of selfless devotees and yogis, is the main stuff of the tale. The fact that he is God and still needs help, however, speaks to his human side.

Lord Rama's humanity is a significant part of the Ramayana, for Ravana was given the boon that he could not be killed by any supernatural being or by the gods in heaven. Thus, Vishnu—the Lord Himself—was approached by the demigods to come down to earth in completely human form, so that Ravana might one day be vanquished by an "ordinary" mortal.[7] Vishnu in the form of Rama responded to their call.

Sita, the divine consort of Lord Rama, is also depicted as being as virtuous as she is beautiful. Indeed, she is seen as an incarnation of Lakshmi, consort of Vishnu, the female manifestation of God. In the Ramayana, Sita is the paradigm of chastity and all that is good and true. Lakshman, Rama's noble brother, selflessly serves the divine couple in all their needs. He is second only to his brother in all of the qualities listed previously. Finally,

Lord Rama, an incarnation of Vishnu, is with his wife
Sita (the Goddess), Lakshman (his brother and first expansion), and Hanuman (his monkey-warrior, friend,
and devotee). © 2003 Mandala Publishing, www.
mandala.org.

Hanuman, the half man/half monkey devotee of Rama, is the very emblem
of strength, chivalry, loyalty, and devotion. It is he who is pivotal in returning Sita to Rama. In some ways, he is the real hero of the Ramayana.[8]

Like the Mahabharata, the Ramayana's climax includes a battle of huge
proportions. This is the fight between Rama's army and that of Ravana, the
obnoxious warlord who had kidnapped Sita. Ultimately, Rama was victorious. With the return of his loving bride, he established the ideal God-
centered kingdom, known in the Indic tradition as Rama Rajya, or "the
Kingdom of Rama," a euphemism still used for nationalistic regimes and
ardent political groups. In the end, after a complex series of events that led
to the banishment of Sita from Rama's ideal kingdom, He concluded his
earthly sojourn and was reunited with her in the Kingdom of God.

THE BHAGAVATA PURANA: THE JEWEL OF INDIA'S WISDOM TEXTS

The Bhagavata Purana, or the Shrimad Bhagavatam, as it is also known, is arguably the best of the 18 Puranas, or the scriptural histories of ancient India. This same work is sometimes called the Bhagavata, which is its abbreviated name. But whatever one calls it, it is a vast and encyclopedic tome, surveying a broad spectrum of knowledge, including history, psychology, politics, cosmology, metaphysics, and theology. In its entirety, it comprises just under 18,000 verses in 12 Cantos, or Books. Most Hindus consider this work to be the essence or highpoint of India's Vedic wisdom.

It was compiled by Vyasa, the same sage who, 50 centuries ago, edited the Vedas and wrote the Mahabharata. Although he had indeed completed these other consequential treatises, by writing the Bhagavata he was responding to a feeling of incompleteness, of despondency. He had presented these feelings before his teacher, Narada, who then told him that in his previous works he had neglected to clearly glorify the name, fame, form, and pastimes of the Lord Himself. His feeling of despondency, said Narada, would subside only if he now rectified that wrong.[9] Thus, he gave the world the Bhagavata Purana.

The primary themes of the Bhagavata are humans' relationship with God, the process of awakening that relationship, and learning how to become absorbed in the goal of that relationship. These three themes are disguised, however, in the exposition of 10 overarching subjects: (1) stories involving the primary creation of the universe, in which earth, water, fire, air, and ether, as well as the total material energy, come into being; (2) the secondary creation, or the work of Brahma, the first created being; (3) the way in which the Lord maintains the universe by His multifarious potencies, with detailed descriptions of how these energies work; (4) the reciprocal relationship between God and His devotee, and the practices designed to promote that relationship; (5) the conditioned soul's impulses for materialistic activities, or the desires that make humankind bound to the material world; (6) the scriptural instructions given to the living beings of this world and the genealogies in which these teachings are found; (7) detailed information about the Personality of Godhead in His various forms; (8) the winding up of all energies in creation; God's potencies are here described with special attention to the destruction of the material universe; (9) the various kinds of liberation, from the cessation of material miseries to perfection in love of God; and (10) the ultimate end of knowledge: the transcendence. The Godhead is described in full, the activities of Krishna, the original Personality of Godhead, being the crown jewels of the Bhagavata's brilliance.

THE BOOK OF MANU

Most Hindus have never actually studied the "Law Code of Manu" (alternatively called Manu-smriti, Manu-samhita, and so on), but it informs most of their day-to-day activities. They tend to learn it haphazardly, through weekly sermons at the temple, parental admonitions, or stray proverbs heard at school. Nonetheless, this work is the most celebrated and honored text outside India's usual corpus of sacred literature. It is considered a "legal" text, with more commentaries than any other book of its kind, and there are many.

The author of this text is unknown, although practitioners tend to believe it is actually Manu, the prehistoric son of Lord Brahma, the first created being. The text itself gives something of its history: Brahma taught it to Manu, who in turn taught it to several qualified pupils, including Bhrigu. It is this highly articulate sage, a disciple of Manu, who proclaims the Lawbook to men and women of this age, and it is his voice we hear in The Book of Manu today. In its present form, the text was composed sometime between the second century B.C.E. and the second century C.E.

As the book opens, a group of sages approaches Manu and ask about duty and law, hoping he will instruct them. He does. He tells them about the creation of the world and its original purpose. Naturally, in due course, he describes the four social classes—intellectuals, warriors, merchants, and workers—and then tells his student, Bhrigu, to explain the rest. As Bhrigu does so, the book goes through the specific duties of each class, along with their expected rituals, marriage customs, food preferences, judicial procedures, forms of taxation, and punishments for various crimes. Unlike earlier texts of this kind, it places undo emphasis on the warrior caste, with an outline of kingly duties, statecraft, and law, perhaps hoping to rectify the growing rift between the intellectuals and administrators of the period.

The most notable aspects of Manu's work, especially in terms of Hinduism as we know it today, include his often sexist treatment of male-female interaction, although this is somewhat tempered by occasional statements that seem to indicate the opposite. Such ambivalence in regard to the treatment of women has filtered down into modern Hindu thinking. Nonetheless, reform movements and counter examples in the Vedic literature make women's rights attainable, even in the most conservative circles. Also noteworthy are Manu's proclamations about vegetarianism. He advocates Vedic sacrifices, even if they include the killing of animals, but he makes clear that eating meat for any other reason is sinful. He asks devotees to think about what is actually involved in animal slaughter, saying that, ultimately, one must suffer a reaction for the killing of animals, even those killed in sacrifice. He goes so far as to say that while vegetarianism is equal to animal sacrifices in terms of the merit procured, the former is preferable, both for the practitioner and, of course, for the slaughtered animals.

ADDITIONAL HINDU TEXTS

Many other texts are used in the study of Hinduism. Of particular importance are a group of works known as Pancharatra, Agama, and Tantra. These three constitute a category of literature used by Vaishnavas (devotees of God in the form of Vishnu), Shaivites (devotees of Shiva, or God for the purpose of universal destruction), and Shaktas (those who revere the Goddess), respectively, although sometimes the words are used interchangeably. They are ritual texts in that they explicate exact procedure for worshiping the divine, although they are not generally philosophical or theological in nature. Rather, they are "how to" manuals for day-to-day activity in relation to God. In some cases, they include esoteric ideas about the spiritual dimension of reality and underlying information about God or the mysteries of the universe.

In addition to these texts, mention must be made of the massive corpus of regional literature throughout the Indian subcontinent. These are usually translations or adaptations of classical Sanskrit scriptures. Most Hindus, in fact, learn their religion through such vernacular versions, despite the special sanctity of the Sanskrit originals. Along these lines, nearly every major region has its own reworking of the great epics, the Ramayana and the Mahabharata, for example, sometimes with considerable variations from the originals.

TENETS: AN OVERVIEW OF HINDU TEACHINGS

Actual Identity and the Path to Liberation

The described texts (and others like them) explain and presuppose certain fundamental theological ideas. These teachings most readily begin with three points: (1) the nature of the living being as a soul and not a body; (2) karma, the law of action and reaction, that is, causality; and (3) reincarnation, the journey of the soul from body to body. These three teachings underscore all Hindu thinking about the nature of reality, and, to properly understand Hinduism, should be looked at in some depth.

In one lifetime, say the Hindu scriptures, an individual passes through many different bodies—infant, child, youth, adult, and so on—but remains the same person. The soul, the entity within the body, does not change; what changes is the body—and only the body (which includes the mind). The person grows, physically, intellectually, emotionally, perhaps spiritually but is still the same living being, the same person. Implicitly, each living entity is an unchanging essence within a material body. To state it in yet another way, the living being is an entity who does not change, while the ever-changing shell with whom—or, more accurately, with which—he or she tends to identify, does change.

The living entity undergoes bodily change based on activities past and present. Actions performed in this body determine the next body, as one's previous actions, in a prior body, determined this one. Thus, Hindu texts assert that the soul's transmigration from body to body does not take place in a random way. Rather, the soul's journey is instigated by subtle desires and by one's karma, or prior actions, whether from earlier in this life or from previous ones.[10] The doctrine of karma is sometimes equated with the biblical precept, "Whatever a man sows, that will he also reap." It is also seen as a metaphysical extension of a physical law: "For every action, there is an equal and commensurate reaction."[11]

It is to accommodate the many possible reactions to any given activity that the various species are created. Each type of body is equipped with a particular sensorial strength, so people can live out their desires and experience their just desserts. In other words, these bodily forms are supposed to accommodate living beings, giving them the necessary facility to enjoy or suffer, as is called for in each case. Ultimately, then, individuals inhabit bodies according to their tastes and desires, which lay at the basis of their actions. For example, most human beings would not say that they wanted to be reborn as an animal. And yet our actions reveal true desires: If a human being is overly inclined to sluggishness and sleep, say the scriptures, the body of a bear, who sleeps for months at a time, might be the right tool for the job. If sex is one's major preoccupation, one might get the body of a pigeon, who mates many times in a day.

Thus, according to Hindu scripture, the soul takes on a succession of bodies as a matter of course, allowing each person to evolve or devolve according to his or her inclination and action. The Bhagavad Gita (2.13) states: "As the embodied soul continuously passes, in this body, from childhood to youth to old age, so, too, does that same soul pass into another body at the time of death." In this way, our various bodies are comparable to a change of clothes, wherein we leave the old ones behind and redress ourselves for new purposes and fresh actions. The clothes change, but the person remains the same. Hindus in the modern era sometimes explain this in terms of the second law of thermodynamics, "the conservation of energy," which states that energy cannot be created or destroyed. If this is so, says the modern Hindu, where does this quantum of energy in the body go at the time of death? The answer, they say, is that it goes to another body, that is, until it resolves its issues and develops love for God, at which point it can return to its original position in the spiritual world.[12]

The entire body/soul philosophy is only a preface to the real purpose of the Hindu texts. The soul is meant to escape rebirth—or the cycle of birth and death—by developing consciousness of God and returning to Him, from whence she comes. Krishna says in the Bhagavad Gita (8.15), "After attaining Me, the great souls … are never born again." Thus, the tradition teaches that the process of religion is meant to free one from material conditioning and from the life of illusion associated with the material world. According to the Brahma-samhita (5.59), "The highest devotion is attained by constant endeavor for self-realization with the help of scriptural evidence, theistic conduct, and perseverance in practice." Krishna states, "From the highest planet in the material world down to the lowest, all are places of misery, wherein repeated birth and death take place. But one who attains to My supreme world [the kingdom of God], will never take birth again" (Bhagavad Gita 8.16).

The Social System of India

The idea of karma, with its system of causality—merits and demerits that follow the living being from body to body—is intimately connected to the social system of ancient India, still used today but in distorted form. Hindu scriptures teach that one is born into this social system, which recognizes a four-tiered division of human endeavor—priestly class (Brahmin), administrative class (Kshatriya), mercantile class (Vaishya), and worker (Shudra)—according to one's prior actions.[13] In other words, the specific family into which one is born is determined by the level of consciousness accrued from previous works, in a previous life.

Once a person is born, however, it must be determined how one's previous conditioning affects one's newly acquired mind and senses. The question then becomes: Will one simply fit the family class into which one is born, or will one become inclined to other work, incorporating new aspects of one's psychophysical make up? The original system was not meant to be rigid, for there are many reasons why one might take birth in a particular family and how one might progress after taking such birth. Krishna himself says in the Bhagavad Gita (4.13) that one's class is to be judged according to inclination, aptitude, and work, which is revealed in due course, not according to birthright. This "nonbirth" consideration is the distinguishing quality between the system described in the scriptures and its modern-day counterpart, the caste system, known as *jati*, a word that literally means "birth."

The original social system is an important part of the epics and the Puranas, the scriptures described previously. Consider, for example, Krishna's instruction to Arjuna, where he tells him to fight the war so central to the Mahabharata narrative. Part of Krishna's argument involves Arjuna's duty as a Kshatriya, or an administrative officer. Had Arjuna been a Brahmin, a priest, Krishna would not have counseled him in the same way. It is not the duty of a priest to fight a war, but Arjuna was a highly qualified officer, and great numbers of innocent people were depending on him to do his duty. Thus, Krishna beckoned him to rise up and to do the needful. In this way, much of one's personal duty (*dharma*)—both religious and social—is determined by one's station in life, and this is a critical doctrine in the practice of Hinduism.

The Guru or Spiritual Preceptor

But how is one to know where one fits in the social scheme of things, or how one should approach God, for that matter? Hinduism teaches the importance of a spiritual master to resolve all such quandaries. In early life, the parents act as *gurus*, or teachers, and give guidance as best they can. But Hindu tradition teaches the importance of associating with genuine saints, or those who have a certain closeness to God. Eventually, teach the scriptures, one who is serious about spiritual life must search out a genuine guru, for, by doing so, one might gain true spiritual knowledge and make genuine progress on the path to transcendence. The analogy given is that of a king's son, or of his intimate servant; if one wants audience with the king, the best way is to associate with his son or his intimate servitor. This will afford opportunities that are otherwise unattainable. Similarly, by their accomplishment and devotion, great practitioners of spiritual life develop an intimacy with God, and by their association—hearing from them and following their instructions—others can develop a similar closeness.

Hindu scriptures are replete with caveats about cheaters in the guise of saints. A genuine spiritual master, says the tradition, rather obviously, must have genuine spiritual knowledge; he must not simply look holy but must actually know and love God. How is a discerning person to know whether a prospective teacher is a fraud? First, there must be a community of practitioners with which one confers. And then the words of the teacher must be checked against the scriptures. An overly creative philosopher and a speculative word juggler are both considered charlatans. To be a guru, one must know the way of the forefathers, the sages, and the tradition. His knowledge must be tested against the previous saints and the scriptures.

In India, too, there are established lineages to which a prospective guru must belong. These lineages pass down the esoteric teachings contained in scripture, and if one learns the scripture outside these lineages, essential truths will necessarily be missed. Serious practitioners of Hinduism, therefore, seek out a teacher who is a respected participant in one of these lineages, and they take initiation to formalize commitment to the spiritual pursuit. At initiation—usually a colorful ceremony, with a fire sacrifice and priests chanting ancient Vedic hymns—one receives a new name, usually a name that in some sense designates one as a servant of God. One also receives a set of beads on which to chant God's names, and a mantra, or a prayer, through which, if one chants sincerely and incessantly, one might find closeness to God. Most important, one receives an opportunity to progress on the spiritual path.

Noninjury to Sentient Beings: Ahimsa

Ahimsa has become a defining characteristic of Hinduism today, and its teaching can be found throughout the Hindu scriptures. Overall, the Hindu tradition is clear on the importance of nonviolence, noninjury, and nonaggression—all synonyms for *ahimsa*—and often takes it to its most far-reaching options, such as animal rights and vegetarianism. The tradition views all life as sacred, and because the body is merely an external shell, we are all living things, whatever our bodily form and are equal in the eyes of God.

This principle has been epitomized in Indian culture by its reverence for the cow. Although the cow is not worshiped as a divine being, as is commonly supposed. Hinduism teaches that the cow should be honored as one of humankind's mothers, because she provides nourishing milk, as does one's mother. All of this points to one essential truth: God sees the soul, the person within, as His intimate servant, as His affectionate child, whom He wants to protect, nurture, and love. And He wants us to interact with each other in this same way. This is a fundamental principle in the Hindu complex of religions.

As an important addendum, The Mahabharata (13.116.37–4), arguably India's greatest epic, says that *ahimsa*, or nonviolence, is the highest duty. This is significant praise, indeed, especially coming from a text in which Krishna, the Supreme Lord, tells his devotee and friend, Arjuna, to engage in battle, killing vast numbers of people on the battlefield of Kurukshetra. This apparent contradiction has perplexed Hindu commentators for centuries. A close study of the scriptures, however, will resolve the dilemma by, again, referring to the social system described previously.

Hindu texts state that a Brahmin (an intellectual or a priest) must practice noninjury carte blanche, without any reservation. But a Kshatriya, or an administrative officer, must sometimes engage in violence to protect people. Such a person, in fact, must define nonviolence a bit differently, looking at a greater good. In fact, if a Kshatriya does not do his or her duty—violent or not—that person becomes guilty of a yet greater crime, causing more harm to a greater number of people. Arjuna's classic example is again the most appropriate. *Ahimsa*, for him, involved protecting the righteous people on the battlefield, which meant harming those who would harm them.

Indian politician and pacifist Mahatma Gandhi wrote that it is sometimes wise to see nonviolence in activities that may externally appear otherwise: "I have come to see that which I did not so clearly see before, that there is sometimes nonviolence in violence.... I had not fully realized the duty of restraining a drunkard from doing evil, or killing a dog in agony or one infected with rabies. In all such instances, violence is in fact nonviolence."[14] Protection from antisocial elements in society, the restraining of wicked persons are virtuous acts, not violence. If an enemy attacks, molests women, or kills innocent people, one who is able to retaliate *must* do so. If not, it is an act of cowardice and weakness. It is certainly not *ahimsa*.

Mahatma Gandhi (1869–1948), famed politician
and spiritual seeker, often known as the father of
modern India. Courtesy of Photofest.

According to the Bhagavad Gita, this principle supersedes any abstraction,
such as unqualified nonviolence (which is often an extremist position),
that, again, may result in more harm done than good.

Theological Diversity

Hinduism is widely known as a tolerant religion. This is not to say that
it accepts all religious doctrines indiscriminately, but it is significantly ac-
commodating, finding a place for almost any conception of spirituality. The
many gods usually associated with the Hindu pantheon, for example, are
seen as various manifestations of the same one God. Although each of these
gods has differing characteristics and express different levels of ultimate reality, the worshippers of these deities are seen as brothers and sisters under
one God. Practitioners of other religions, too, are seen as brothers and sisters. Thus, according to Hindu teachings, there is only one God in heaven,
regardless of what we call Him (or Her) or what forms He (or She) takes.

Because Hinduism recognizes diverse aspects of God, in diverse forms, it is sometimes viewed as polytheistic, or believing in many gods. However, these "many gods" are simply a manifestation of how God descends in an infinity of ways—sometimes manifesting His full power and identity, and, by way of various gradations, manifesting in lesser or incomplete forms as well. There is no end to the varieties of forms with which He reciprocates the love of His devotees. For example, He exists in His original kingdom, in the spiritual world, and He also has a "Universal Form," which essentially comprises the entire material cosmos. Practitioners who accentuate this latter form favor animism, or seeing God in nature. He also manifests as the Deity, a visible image made of earth, wood, marble, gold, and so on. This is an iconic form that is worshiped according to strict rules and regulations, in one's home or in a temple. The tradition also says that He comes to earth in so many incarnations (*avataras*), the most important of which are all mentioned in the scriptures, and here He specifically interacts with humankind for specific purposes of His own. God manifests as the many demigods, or highly empowered beings, too, and as certain sages, who help humanity in multifarious ways.

Chiefly, three aspects of the divine are accentuated in the Hindu scriptures: (1) Brahman, God's all-pervading and formless aspect; (2) the Supersoul, His aspect as the "Lord in the heart" (although here He is not to be confused with the individual living entity, also residing in the region of the heart), who exists within each living entity, and in and between every atom; and (3) Bhagavan, His aspect as the Supreme Person. These three aspects are seen as equal, in that they refer to the same Absolute Truth. But there is simultaneously a hierarchy, with the personal form of Bhagavan, the Supreme Person, at the top. The hierarchy exists because each successive stage of God realization includes the prior one, that is to say, one who attains Supersoul realization will necessarily have achieved Brahman realization as well. And one who realizes Bhagavan, the Supreme Person, has also perceived the truths found in Brahman and Supersoul.

The impersonal aspect of the Lord is generally approached by the contemplative meditator, the one who renounces the world to pursue spiritual knowledge. The Supersoul aspect is generally the domain of the *yogi*, or the serious practitioner of severe penances and austerities, following the many rules and regulations of *yoga* practice as delineated in the scriptures.[15] Finally, the Personality of Godhead is pursued by the devotee, the loving servant of God who anxiously seeks to reclaim his lost relationship with Him.

The Path to God

The whole of Hindu religion is constructed in such a way as to foster a methodical mood of devotion (bhakti), wherein one can develop loving sentiments for God according to an almost scientific procedure. For example, the Supreme Person is approached in two ways: (1) with awe and reverence or (2) with loving intimacy. Both are considered legitimate, even if the second of the two is considered superior, and there are detailed scriptural instructions on how to pursue either one. In pursuance of God in either of these ways, guidelines and bench marks are delineated in the scriptures, so that one might gauge whether or not one is making advancement on the spiritual path.

There are eight levels of advancement highlighted by the scriptures. Dispensing with the complex Sanskrit terminology that defines these levels, the first is called simply *faith*. This kind of faith is not blind but based on experiential knowledge. It is achieved by adhering to certain basic principles of purification, by associating with those who have already fully imbibed the qualities and knowledge of the scriptures, and by studying the scriptures themselves. One can quickly graduate from this level by *regularly associating with saints*. Here one finds a teacher and a community of devotees with whom one develops intimate relationships. By this powerful association, one finds that saintly qualities become accessible, and one becomes more fully interested and even acclimated to the behaviors and patterns of spiritual life.

The third level is called *engagement in worship*. While attempting various spiritual practices, one undergoes tension in progressing from neophyte to seasoned practitioner, from unsteadiness to steadiness. The enthusiasm with which one initially approached the spiritual path is now naturally tested in numerous ways. There is an unevenness in one's ability to be attentive while offering prayers, for example, leading to failure on the spiritual path, or, if one passes the test, intensifying conviction and concentration. At this stage, one generally falls away from serious practice or makes a commitment to the path and receives initiation from a spiritual preceptor (*guru*).

The fourth level, *cessation of unwanted elements* comes next. By serious practice, over the course of time, one sees the decimation of all one's unwanted habits and material conditioning. One gradually becomes cleansed of base instinct and material desires, now wanting more than ever the fruit of love of God. As this level enhances one's resolve, one becomes *steady*, the fifth level, in the pursuit of the goal. This much coveted level of steadiness is attained after overcoming a good deal of deeply rooted distraction, doubt, conditioning, and the influence of sensual pleasures. At this point, few obstacles can deter the spiritual aspirant from the practice of devotion.

Steadiness leads to the sixth level, *taste*. Here one develops a clearly defined inclination for things of the spirit. One wants to rise early and pray, to chant with conviction, to worship the deity—all the practices that one had previously performed out of a sense of obligation or commitment now become desirable, even a passionate preoccupation. One's conditional responses and tastes are now palpably changed, and one becomes naturally absorbed in the goal. From this comes level seven, *attachment*. Here one develops the natural inclination to guard one's spiritual life as one's most precious gift. And God becomes one's life and soul. Whereas in the previous stage, the *path* was the all-encompassing meditation, here it transfers from path to *goal*, from practice to spontaneous devotion for God. Here there is less need for endeavor, because, out of attachment, one's focus becomes an impulse, or second nature.

For those who are extremely perseverant, the next level, eight, is called *intense emotion*. At this stage, the soft heart of the now experienced practitioner melts like butter when left in a warm area, and a deep feeling of sweetness overtakes one's relationship with God. An unquenchable yearning for meeting the Lord is now perpetually present in one's heart, leading to level nine, *ecstatic love*—the fruit of one's practice, self-realization, or realization of exactly who one is in the spiritual world, in relationship to God. Moreover, one becomes ensconced in this higher identity, even while still in this world, and gains vision of the Lord. Such a perfected practitioner is given to sacred rapture, transcendental ecstasy, and the joy of being in proximity to the spiritual element. At the height of such perfection, the devotee relishes the supreme joy of love of God, a love that is described as increasing at every moment.

The World of Illusion: Maya

The concept of illusion (*maya*) is central to Hindu thought. "That which is not" and "that which is measurable" are among the many definitions of the word *maya*, although literally (and in most ancient Vedic texts) it simply refers to "*magic*." *Maya* is thus identified as the material world, for things of this world are temporary and measurable as well. The spiritual element, by contrast, exists eternally and cannot be measured.

Certain schools of traditional Hindu philosophy deem the material world to be an illusion and nothing more, but the early Vaishnava schools asserted that the material world is not an illusion in toto. Rather, it is *illusory* in the sense of being temporary; it exists, but it does not *continue to exist*. Like a dream, then, the material world has some temporary meaning, some substance in the life of the person who does the dreaming; but like all dreams, it comes to an end.

Maya is also understood in terms of a rope and a snake: Both exist, but if a person confuses one for the other, *that* is illusion. Enlightenment, for the Hindu, involves being able to separate reality from illusion, to overcome the phantasmagoria of the material world and to see reality for what it is.

Spiritual Fellowship: Satsang

Hindus place a premium on associating with people who are serious about the spiritual path. They are generally not concerned with whether one claims affiliation with one particular group or another, but rather with the intensity of one's spiritual practice. That being said, devotees of any particular group will usually congregate mainly with devotees of the same lineage.

To this end, temples are usually meeting grounds for practitioners of like mind. Together, they will sing, dance, worship, and study. Devotional principles include revealing one's mind to other practitioners, allowing them to reveal their minds in return, exchanging gifts with others, and giving in charity. These are deemed healthy acts for one's psychological, emotional, and, most important, spiritual development.

Practitioners are encouraged to view neophytes as those to be helped and guided, equals to be befriended, and superiors to be learned from and to be assisted in their worship. Most Hindu groups teach that spiritual advancement is quite difficult in a vacuum. Rather, by the association of those whose hearts contain the proper spiritual ingredients, one can attain proper nourishment in love of God.

Morals and Ethics

Although Hinduism is not generally known for its pronounced view on morals and ethics, it stands alongside the Judeo-Christian tradition in support of right conduct and altruistic behavior. The bedrock of Judeo-Christian ethics, for example, is found in the Golden Rule: "Do unto others as you would have others do unto you" (Matthew 7.12). The Mahabharata (5.15.17), India's great epic, shares the same sentiments: "This is the sum of duty: Do not do to others that which would cause pain if done to you."[16]

In Hinduism, there is also a set of teachings that correspond to the Ten Commandments. These are called Yamas and Niyamas, which are basically a list of "dos" and "don'ts."

1. *Ahimsa,* described already, is the first "do" on the positive side of the list: Be nonviolent in thought and action, and avoid arrogance and anger.
2. One must tell the truth—to refrain from lying and making good on one's promises. This also involves avoiding injustice.
3. The command not to steal or covet is central to Hindu ethics. Here it also involves respecting another's property.
4. One must endeavor to relinquish one's lust; this is often taken to the point of celibacy but at least includes sexual restraint to some degree.
5. The effort to discipline desire and greed is fundamental to all Hindu traditions.
6. Cleanliness is next to godliness, in Hinduism as elsewhere. This commandment encourages practitioners to be pure in body, mind, and speech.
7. There is a mandate to be peaceful, to appreciate one's lot in life, to be satisfied with whatever God gives.
8. One must develop a sense of penance, sacrifice, or austerity. These are seen as virtues that, when properly motivated, are always advantageous to spiritual life.
9. Education is seen as the gateway to higher knowledge. All Hindu traditions support the injunction to study the scriptures and assorted books of wisdom.
10. Above everything else, one must cultivate devotion to God through daily worship and meditation. True devotion also involves giving to others without ulterior motive.

The Cyclical Nature of Reality and the Rotating System of Self-Realization

Hindus see reality in terms of cycles. Like the hands on a clock, the rising and setting of the sun, or the seasons of the year, all reality exists in a state of perpetual recurrence. In the process of reincarnation, for example, wherein the soul undergoes birth and death, and which, in turn, lead to rebirth and the whole process all over again, the Hindu sees the greater time cycle in terms of world ages. In Greek philosophical and historical texts, these ages—from beginning to end—are referred to as the Golden, Silver, Copper, and Iron Ages.

Similarly, Hindu texts teach that there are four ages beginning in a golden, that is, virtuous, atmosphere. Gradually, however, time causes devolution, and the ages are said to degenerate in terms of goodness and in terms of the spiritual acumen of the people.

By the time of our current age, which, by Hindu reckoning, began 5,000 years ago, people are short-lived, quarrelsome, lazy, and always disturbed. More, there is a tendency to be distracted from spiritual life.

This rather dismal view of contemporary society is counterbalanced by progressively easier and more effective means of self-realization. In the first age, for example, when people were spiritually inclined and had many virtuous qualities, they could achieve the Lord only through intense meditation, the rigors of which would cause failure for many today. The following age allowed practitioners to reach this same goal through elaborate ritual sacrifices of the Vedic kind, which, although difficult, were considerably easier than training the mind in the complexities of meditation. The third age was easier still, for now beautiful temples were built in honor of the Lord and practitioners could reach Him through heartfelt prayers at the temple and the elaborate worship of the Deity form who resides there.

As stated, the fourth and final age is distinguished by the profound disqualifications of those who live in it. According to Hindu scriptures, however, God complements these disqualifying times with an extremely powerful method for realizing Him, attempting to compensate for the difficulties of the current age. He asks one only to call out to Him with love and devotion, to chant His name with sincerity and purpose. The philosophical underpinnings of this "sonic theology" are not as simple as they might at first sound.[17] The basic idea is that God and His name are nondifferentiated. God, being absolute in nature, is not subject to differentiation; every aspect of His being contains the essence of every other aspect. Thus, His form is equal to His pastimes, which is equal to His name, and so on. The material world is just the opposite. A given material phenomenon and the word that's used to describe it are inherently different. If one chants "water, water, water," for example, one's thirst will not be quenched. Conversely, if one chants "Vishnu, Vishnu, Vishnu," especially under the direct guidance of one who has mastered the process, one is put in direct touch with God.

Thus, that which was once obtainable only through grueling meditation, elaborate ritual sacrifice, or gorgeous temple worship, requiring untold riches and fanfare, can now be had by heartfelt praise alone. As Krishna says in the Padma Purana, one of Hinduism's sacred scriptures: "In this age, I dwell not in the spiritual kingdom, nor in the hearts of yogis—only where My devotees chant My name, there, you should know, is where I stand!"

NOTES

1. The epics and the Puranas are the main texts of contemporary Hinduism, although there are many others. Most important among these, perhaps, is the Vedanta-sutra, terse codes that summarize all of Vedic philosophy, and also the Tiruvaymoli, or the "Tamil Veda." For more on this latter work, see Vasudha Narayanan, *The Vernacular Veda* (Columbia: University of South Carolina Press, 1994).

2. The Vedas were originally studied only by learned male priests, who were accomplished in Sanskrit and who had the spiritual acumen to understand the esoteric rituals prescribed there. The books were denied to other factions of society. Not so for the secondary literature known as the Fifth Veda and its corollaries. These works broke open the spiritual storehouse of Vedic knowledge for the masses, explaining not only the philosophy behind the rituals but also recasting them in terms of new rites and procedures.

3. The Mahabharata's proclamation of itself as the fifth Veda might appear self-serving, as might similar claims made by several of the Puranas, or the established history books of ancient India. After all, the Veda is identified with direct revelation, and, therefore, any literature directly associated with it will automatically garner divine status. Nevertheless, there are quotations from within the Vedic corpus itself that legitimate the claims made by the Mahabharata and the Puranas. For example, Atharva Veda 11.7.24, Chandogya Upanishad 7.1.4, and the Brihadaranyaka Upanishad 2.4.10 all suggest that the epics and the Puranas are part of the original Vedic literature.

4. This bold claim is found near the beginning of the Mahabharata's central narrative and again toward the end of it (at 1.56.33 and at 18.5.38, respectively), underlining Vyasa's confidence that, indeed, all things are found in the epic's pages.

5. The word *caste* is used here for convenience. Actually, the original socioreligious system of ancient India, known as Varnashrama, was applied to individuals according to their intrinsic quality and vocational inclination. The contemporary caste system, on the other hand, is based on birth (*jati*), identifying one's status according to family heritage and social hierarchy.

6. Krishna is considered by most Hindus to be an incarnation of Vishnu, the Supreme Lord. However, the Bhagavata Purana (1.3.27), the Brahma-samhita (5.1), and other Vaishnava texts clearly grant a unique place to Krishna as the source of all Vishnu forms. Several Vaishnava groups who heed these texts, therefore, are more aptly called forms of Krishnaism than Vaishnavism, as their emphasis is on Krishna as the "Supreme Personality of Godhead." Traditional

groups with this perspective include the Gaudiya and Vallabha lineages, as well as the modern-day Hare Krishna movement.

7. Rama's appearance as a fully human manifestation of the Supreme Being inevitably evokes thoughts of Jesus, who, in the Christian tradition, is similarly viewed as God in human form.

8. However, in India, Hanuman is sometimes divinized, which goes against the text of the Ramayana. According to the scripture, he is clearly the devotee, not the Lord, a position held exclusively for Rama.

9. Narada's reprimand of Vyasa is found in the Bhagavata 1.5.8–9, 13.

10. The doctrine of karma has been criticized, even within the tradition itself, for embodying a sense of fatalism, or resignation to destined reaction. This criticism, however, is ill conceived, and if one actually studies what the ancient texts say about karma it becomes clear that all action and its concomitant reaction can be abrogated by devotion to God, as explained in the Bhagavad Gita. So although each individual's present is indeed determined by his or her past, each can still influence the future by conducting himself or herself in a spiritual manner.

11. Not unlike the intelligentsia of other established religions, Hindus in the modern era seek to substantiate their beliefs with the findings of modern science. Here we find Newton's third law of motion, "For every action, there is an equal and opposite reaction," called on. For more on this, see Richard Thompson, *God and Science: Divine Causation and the Laws of Nature* (Alachua, Fla.: Govardhana Hill Publishing, 2004).

12. Ibid.

13. India's social system is integrally related to a spiritual system, traditionally followed by the three upper classes, the Brahmins, Kshatriyas, and Vaishyas. This refers to celibate students (Brahmacharis), the married couples who pursue spiritual life together (Grihasthas), those who gradually retire from married life to more fully engage in spiritual practices (Vanaprasthas), and renunciants, who give up all material ties and devote the entire remainder of their life to spiritual pursuits (Sannyasis).

14. Trivedi, Mark, *Mohandas Gandhi: The Man and His Vision* (Calcutta, India: Time Publications, 1968), p. 10.

15. *Yoga* literally means "to unite with God." The contemporary fascination with yoga in the West stems from one small part of the traditional yogic regimen as outlined in the Hindu scriptures: the exercises that make for a firm body and mind, which are supposed to then be used in the spiritual pursuit. It is questionable whether most yoga practitioners in the West use their enhanced bodies for this purpose.

16. In wording the commandment in its negative form, that is, "Do *not* do unto others ... " rather than *"Do* unto others ... ," the Mahabharata is more in league with the Jewish version of the Golden Rule found in the Talmud (*Shabbat,* 31a). In either case, the spirit of morals and ethics is basically the same.

17. See Guy L. Beck, *Sonic Theology: Hinduism and Sacred Sound* (Columbia: University of South Carolina Press, 1993).

3

BRANCHES

Hinduism is a conglomerate of numerous religious traditions, so there is no central trunk from which branches grow. That being said, the Vedic tradition, complete with its earliest literature, known as the four Vedas, and the secondary literature, such as the epics and the Puranas (see Chapter 2), might be considered the root; thus all traditions growing out of this foundation could be seen as branches of Hinduism. Thus, India's many "Hindu" religions are, in a sense, branches. This begins with the large, overarching traditions—Vaishnavism, the worship of God in the form of Vishnu or any of His many incarnations and expansions; Shaivism, the worship of Shiva, Lord of destruction; and Shaktism, the veneration of the Goddess, known as Kali, Durga, Uma, and so on. Other branches are found in the many minor religious traditions in India. This chapter outlines the three major branches along with some of its subsects, which can, to extend the analogy, be considered twigs, or, in some cases, the very fruit of the Vedic tree of knowledge.

VAISHNAVISM: WORSHIP OF VISHNU

Widely considered the most significant Hindu tradition today—certainly in terms of numbers and arguably in terms of complexity—Vaishnavism is a monotheistic tradition that centers on the worship of Vishnu, the "Oversoul" of the universe. Vishnu exists in numerous forms, such as Krishna and Rama, and, for this reason, the religion is often viewed as polytheistic; the various forms of Vishnu are mistakenly seen as many different gods. Nonetheless, a close study reveals that his plentiful manifestations are like so many facts on a precious gem; it is *one* gem, no matter how many facets it might have. In general, the Hindu conception of divinity is multifaceted, and Vaishnavism is no exception: "The Divine is a diamond of innumerable facets; two very large and bright facets are Vishnu and Shiva, while the others represent all the gods that were ever worshipped. Some facets seem larger, brighter, and better polished than others, but in fact the devotee.... worships the whole diamond, which is in reality perfect."[1]

This is not to say that all the gods are equal, or that they partake of the same level of divinity. Indeed, the Vedic literature goes to great pains to reveal a hierarchy of divine beings, and although from one level of perception, these gods are one, they are also many. This is a truth found in the earliest of Vedic aphorisms.

Despite this simultaneous "oneness and difference" among the gods of India, Vishnu has received special attention from the earliest strata of Vedic literature. Although he is mentioned but a few times in the original Veda, as one among many divinities, the significance of these references has not gone unnoticed.[2] He is described as all-pervasive in a way that the other gods are not. He is further identified with the holy sacrifices of the Vedas, sacrifices that were somehow mystically identified with God Himself.[3] And, by the time of the Mahabharata and the Puranas, the epics and ancient histories, respectively—literature that tradition attributes to roughly 50 centuries ago—he is seen as the Supreme Godhead.[4] In general, modern Hinduism acknowledges his paramount ranking among the gods, even if many practitioners see him as somehow coalescing with the others. The ability to distinguish one god from the other—to consider who is supreme and who is a lesser god, like an angel or simply an empowered living entity from a higher planet—is, again, the prerogative of the priestly class and those trained in the esoteric traditions.

Vishnu's Form

Unlike the image of God portrayed in other religious traditions, particularly in the West, Vishnu's form leaves little to the imagination. He is often depicted as lying down in the causal ocean, far beyond the material sphere; sometimes, he is sitting, or standing, with his feminine counterpart Lakshmi, the Goddess of Fortune. This Goddess is often depicted, in narrative traditions, as one of his two wives (the other goes by the name Bhudevi). Obviously, these feminine divinities are not "wives" in the usual sense of the term. Ultimately, they are manifestations of Vishnu's spiritual and ma-

Lord Buddha, also known as Siddhartha Gautama, is seen by Hindus as an incarnation of Vishnu, or God, as he is envisioned by the Vaishnavas. © 1998 Mandala Publishing, www.mandala.org.

terial energy, respectively. He and his lovely female counterparts evoke an image of a spiritual world that is populated by the Lord in many different features, for he expands to relish intimate relationships. In addition to his own divine forms—including his direct expansions and his female counterparts—his kingdom is inhabited by countless spiritual entities, each engaging in his divine service with the deepest love and affection.

Vishnu's majestic, imposing visage—more than any other form in that spiritual kingdom—arouses awe and reverence. His jet black hair, lotus eyes, and sky blue complexion are highlighted by his golden dress, jewelry embellishments, and stately features. He has four arms, indicating his omnipresence and omnipotence. In his right hand he holds the discus, the ultimate weapon—a reminder of the wheel of time. His other right hand wields the conch shell, symbol of the clarion call of truth, justice, and victory. In his left hand he gently clasps a lotus flower, representing good fortune, beauty, eternity, prosperity, and purity. And in his lower left hand he embraces a mace, with which he protects his devotees.

Vishnu takes many forms. Initially, there are three: Karanodakashayi Vishnu, the original Vishnu who appears in the kingdom of God; he expands into Garbhodakashayi Vishnu, the Lord of the Universe, who enters into the material world, giving it a sense of divinity and life; and then there is Kshirodakashayi Vishnu, a further expansion that animates all that is, entering into the hearts of all living beings (although still distinct from these beings) and into the stuff of material existence.

In the material world, Vishnu manifests in an infinity of forms, but his 10 most famous incarnations are:

1. The Divine Fish, Matsya, who saved the world from a deluge recorded in ancient Vedic texts.
2. The Divine Tortoise, Kurma, who offered his back as the pivot on which Mt. Mandara rested. Here, gods and demons both churned various valuable objects from the ocean of milk, a famous story from the Vedic literature.
3. The Boar, Varaha, like Matsya, rescued the earth from a flood, raising it from watery depths on his tusk, for otherwise it would have been completely submerged.
4. The Man-Lion, Narasimha, came to earth to deliver the world from a demon, who had obtained from the gods a boon stating that he would be slain neither by a god, human, nor animal. Narasimha was not any of these, for he was a combination of all of them.
5. The Dwarf, Vamana, was Vishnu in the form of a dwarf. Here he was confronted with a demon king who had conquered the universe. On behalf of humankind, he begged from the demon for as much land as he could cover in three steps. His request was granted, but, much to the demon king's surprise, Vamana traversed the universe in these three steps, winning the world back for those who are righteous.
6. Rama with the axe, Parashurama, was Vishnu in the form of a hero. Here he destroyed the warrior class of men, who were exploiting others with their power.
7. Ramachandra, the great hero of the Hindu odyssey, the Ramayana (see Chapter 2), taught, by his own example, the true meanings of fidelity, love, and duty.
8. Krishna, the playful lord of Vraja, is often viewed as the most perfect incarnation of Vishnu, and even as the source of all incarnations. He displays his charming *lila*, or divine actions, to allure humanity back to the transcendental realm.
9. Buddha, the founder of Buddhism, is seen as an incarnation of Vishnu as well, although his primary accomplishment, according to Vaishnava texts, is that he bewilders those inclined to atheism. By doing so, say the Vaish-

nava sages, He gradually gets them to abandon harmful habits (such as meat eating) and to once again adopt Vedic teaching in earnest.[5]

10. Kalki is the form of Vishnu who comes at the end of the present age, in about 427,000 years. At that time, all devotees will already be reunited with Vishnu in his heavenly kingdom. The remaining souls, whose lives, according to Hindu texts, are unfortunate, shortened, and riddled with disease, will be mercifully slain by Vishnu so that they might be reborn in the next Satya Age, a pious time when the world is once again created anew.[6]

According to tradition, incarnations and manifestations of Vishnu are as abundant as the waves of an ocean. Nonetheless, when considering these multitudinous aspects of the Supreme, there are two things to bear in mind. First, these incarnations and manifestations represent various sides of one overarching divinity; they are not many gods, as previously stated. Second, the various forms of Vishnu are carefully delineated in the scriptures. The scriptures cannot explicitly name all of the untold incarnations and manifestations, so these texts describe symptoms and definitive signs of divinity. By being attentive to these symptoms, practitioners can avoid being duped. Nonetheless, most people do not rigorously study their sacred texts, and therefore they might assign divinity to personalities who would otherwise be rejected by scriptural standards.

Krishna, although often appearing in lists of incarnations like the one outlined previously, is generally seen as the source of all incarnations, especially in particular Vaishnava schools of thought, such as those of Bengal, or Vraja, in northern India. As the Bhagavata Purana, the cream of ancient India's literary traditions, puts it: "While all of these incarnations are parts, or parts of parts, of the Supreme Lord, Krishna is God Himself."[7] He is the essence of divinity, and yet he is accessible, offering intimacy and relationship for all who desire it.

The tradition paints a clear picture of this topmost manifestation of the Divine. Krishna (Sanskrit for "black" or "dark blue") has a hauntingly beautiful complexion that is usually compared to a dark rain cloud or to deep blue sapphire—hence, his name. He is envisioned as an alluring cowherd, known as Govinda ("leader of cows"), frolicking happily with his divine friends in a bucolic atmosphere. His face, eyes, hands, and feet are frequently compared to lotus flowers, both because of their softness and their general loveliness. Particularly lovely are his large and perfectly formed eyes, the quintessence of beauty, which shine with wisdom and playfulness at the same time. His curling locks of raven black hair is crowned by a peacock feather, and his lips are usually adorned with a bamboo flute, with which he calls all souls back to their spiritual origins.

Lord Krishna, the emporium of love, regarded as the
essence of spiritual truth and the highest divinity. ©
2003 Mandala Publishing, www.mandala.org.

His feminine counterpart Radha, the most enchanting of his cowherd
girlfriends, is the original creative energy of the universe. She is an alternate manifestation of Vishnu's Goddess in more approachable form—the
embodiment of bliss, the very heart of Krishna's essence. She is the inner
beauty of love itself, and although she is actually one with Krishna, she
manifests separately both to bring him pleasure and to bestow mercy on
all living beings.

The relationship of Radha and Krishna has been a focal point in Vaishnava religion. Often criticized by outsiders as appearing overly erotic, the
interrelation of these deities should be understood in terms of otherworldly
love and spiritual exchange. It is clearly not a story of carnal appetite and
prurient interest. Noteworthy in this regard is the fact that the same sacred texts that describe their "sensual" interaction also take great pains to
establish their divinity. A prime example of this is Jayadeva's Gita Govinda,
the twelfth-century text that popularized the love of Radha and Krishna.
Here, the author devotes the entire opening chapter to Krishna's identifica-

Radha and Krishna: The Supreme Lord as lover par excellence and as beloved par excellence. © 2003 Mandala Publishing, www. mandala.org.

tion with Vishnu and thus with the Supreme Deity. Only after prefacing his work with this important point does he proceed to expound on the love play of Radha and Krishna.

This is the great mystery of Krishna, who appeared on earth 5,000 years ago but who exists eternally in the celestial Vraja, the highest portion of heaven—the kingdom of God. It is said that his manifestation meets every human need: As a divine child, he satisfies humankind's urge for giving warmth, fulfilling a maternal instinct to nurture others; as a divine lover, he fulfills romantic fantasies, sweeping practitioners off their feet; as a charioteer in the Mahabharata, the great epic, he is a hero who helps all who come to him with love and devotion. Indeed, what Vishnu offers to those who prefer to approach God with awe and reverence, Krishna offers to those who favor love.[8]

CENTRAL FEATURES OF VAISHNAVISM

Some important aspects of Vaishnava religion in general are the following:

1. It sees itself not as a sectarian religion but as Sanatana Dharma, or the eternal function of the soul. In other words, all religions are but various expressions of Vaishnavism, to greater or lesser degrees. The soul is by nature an eternal servant of Vishnu (or Krishna, Rama, Allah, Jehovah, and/or other manifestations of God, depending on the lineage, tradition, or religion with which one identifies).

2. God manifests variously—as an impersonal abstraction, as the soul of the universe, and as the Supreme Person in His spiritual kingdom. He also appears in deity form, that is, as the image worshiped in the temple, and He often interacts with humankind as so many incarnations (*avataras*); that is, He periodically descends into the world of three dimensions and manifests His confidential spiritual activities for all to see. His motivation for appearing in this latter form is twofold: (a) He comes to unburden the world of evil by personally killing particularly powerful demons and (b) He attracts the pious by His wonderful feats of love and sweetness.

3. Krishna, or Vishnu (or one of His direct incarnations), is the Supreme form of Godhead.

4. Vishnu possesses infinite and multifarious energies, which are briefly mentioned in the world's sacred literature but are more fully described in the Vedic and Puranic texts of ancient India.

5. The souls of this world are part of Vishnu's energies—they are technically called his "separated parts"—and their proper function is to serve him and to develop love for him.

6. Certain souls are engrossed in Vishnu's illusory energy, which is considered his "material energy" (*maya*). By the practice of Vaishnavism, they can free themselves from the grip of such all-encompassing illusion.

7. All spiritual and material phenomena are simultaneously one with and yet different from the Lord.

8. Krishna, among all manifestations of Vishnu, is an ocean of intimacy, and one can derive the highest bliss by becoming reestablished in one's eternal relationship with him, which is now dormant.[9]

9. "Devotional service" (*bhakti-yoga*) is the mystical path by which one can enter into a relationship with God. It supersedes all pious action, the cultivation of knowledge, and various mystical endeavors, such as yoga and meditation (although in its practice it subsumes various forms of yogic mysticism). The science of this holy devotion is detailed in books such as the Bhagavad Gita and the Bhagavata Purana, but it is chiefly understood by associating with devotees who carry it in their hearts. The central practices of this path include singing the praises of God, chanting His names in a regulated fashion, offering food to Him as a sacrament of devotion, and worshiping His image in the temple or in one's home.

10. Pure love of God is alone the ultimate fruit of the spiritual journey.[10]

Vaishnava Lineage and Its Luminaries

Vaishnava teaching is passed down in esoteric lineages (see Chapter 1). These lineages are called *sampradayas*, and there are basically four: the Brahma Sampradaya, the Sri Sampradaya, the Rudra Sampradaya, and the Kumara Sampradaya. These four eventually sprouted into many others, offshoots that claim legitimization based on their connection to these standard traditions. The initial four, however, remain the most prestigious because of their prehistoric origin and the divinities who stand at their base.

Although the original lineages are deemed ancient, they were systematized around 1000 C.E., some before, some later, by four consequential teachers who lived their lives in exemplary Vaishnava ways and whose scriptural learning remains unsurpassed. This began early on with Vishnusvami (born ca. 700 C.E.), who affiliated with the Rudra lineage. Then came Ramanuja (1017–1137 C.E.), the renowned teacher of the Sri lineage. He based his writings on the ideas of the Alvars, 12 poet-saints whose intense devotion for God epitomized the teachings of Vaishnavism. Next came Nimbarka (ca. 1100 C.E.), who represented the Kumara lineage. And then there was Madhva (1199–1278 C.E.) of the Brahma lineage, who was a revolutionary among Vaishnavas because whereas most Vaishnava traditions acknowledged that living beings are both the same as God (in that both God and the living beings are spiritual entities) and different from Him (in that God is great and the living beings are small), Madhva taught that living beings are different from God—period—without any sense of sameness. God, for Madhva, was totally Other. This, of course, was acknowledged by the other lineages as well, but each line of thought had its own particular emphasis.

One way to remember the most important Vaishnava teachers and their particular slant on the tradition's teachings is as follows: Shankara, an eighth-century mystic who viewed God as formless, *denied* all difference between the living entity and God. All entities, he said, are but manifestations of the supreme living entity, with no substantial differences. The various Vaishnava schools reacted to this viewpoint. First, Ramanuja *detected* the differences between God and the living entity. Madhva then *emphasized* the difference. And Sri Chaitanya, who is elaborated on later, *harmonized* the difference. In this way, the various Vaishnava schools of thought promote different visions regarding humankind's relationship with God. These are the main branches of Vaishnava thought.

The systematizers mentioned here began a Vaishnava renaissance, reaching a high point in the twelfth century. This can be deduced from the highly esoteric literature of that period, such as the poetry of Vidyapati and

Chandidas, and, not least, the Gita Govinda of Jayadeva Goswami. Here was a body of work, masterfully crafted and beautifully written, that delved into the underlying themes and philosophical implications of devotion to Krishna. More confidential and intimate than any religious literature before that time, this work set the stage for the blossoming of a deeply contemplative tradition that celebrated God in personal terms that took the sentiments of love and relationship and applied them with full force to the divine.

All of this culminated in the appearance of Sri Chaitanya Mahaprabhu (1486–1533 C.E.), already mentioned, the devotional ecstatic-saint believed by his followers to be a particularly resplendent incarnation of Krishna. Sri Chaitanya's Bhakti ("devotional") movement, in which he captured the very essence of India's spiritual culture, is considered by many to be the cap on the Vaishnava tradition, giving it the gusto and emotional intensity for which it is known today. Despite having been initiated in the Brahma-Madhva lineage, Sri Chaitanya is generally seen as having founded his own tradition, known variously as Chaitanya Vaishnavism, Bengali Vaishnavism, and Gaudiya Vaishnavism. The modern-day Hare Krishna movement, which is explored at length here is a contemporary expression of this form of Vaishnavism.

Vallabha (1479–1531 C.E.) lived around the same time as Chaitanya, and he founded one of the other important Vaishnava branches of northern India, the Vallabha lineage, which claims a connection with Vishnuswami, and thus with the Rudra succession of teachers. Whereas Chaitanya's school of thought emphasizes attachment to God in the mood of conjugal love, the Vallabha branch more emphasizes loving God as a parent loves her child. These approaches to divine love are described scientifically, with elaborate and sophisticated nuance, in the sacred texts of India and also in the regional literature associated with these Vaishnava traditions.

Although there are many other important teachers and denominations of these various lineages—and outside these lineages—mention must be made of certain later luminaries in the line of Ramanuja, for here we encounter two important branches of Vaishnava Hinduism. This refers specifically to the Sri lineage. Here, two distinct schools emerged in thirteenth-century India, eventually leading to a split in the eighteenth century, forming two groups known as the Tenkalai ("southern") and the Vatakalai ("northern"). The founding fathers of these two branches were Manavalama Muni (1370–1443) and Vedanta Deshika (1270–1369), respectively.

These two highly intellectual stalwarts of the Vaishnava tradition conceived of approaching God in one of two ways, known as the "cat and monkey disparity."[11] The Tenkalai, under the direction of Manavalama Muni, say that God saves the soul in the same way that a mother cat transports her kitten. The mother cat makes all the effort, while the kitten remains passive, submissively carted to various locations in the mother's mouth. In contradistinction to this, the Vatakalai, represented by Vedanta Deshika, say that God functions like a mother monkey carrying *her* baby. Although the mother is doing most of the work, the baby must play her part by holding on, arms wrapped around the mother's neck and legs around her back.

This theological dispute has its counterpart in the Christian tradition, where it is referred to as the "grace and works" dichotomy. There, Catholics tend to opt for a "monkey school" position, where the soul must perform good works and play its part to receive the grace of God, whereas Protestantism has traditionally leaned toward the "cat school," saying that all salvation comes only by the grace of God, without human effort. Most Christians say it is a combination of both grace and works, and most Vaishnavas would say the same.

SHAIVISM: THE VENERATION OF LORD SHIVA

Shaivism, or the worship of Lord Shiva ("the Auspicious One"), is another prominent branch of Hinduism. Although Shiva is seen in the Vaishnava tradition as both an alternate manifestation of Vishnu in charge of universal destruction and as Vishnu's greatest devotee, Shaivites see him as God, without any qualifying afterthought.[12] The worshipers of Shiva tend to give Vishnu a lower seat, or, at best, consider him an aspect of their cherished Deity.

Shiva, like Vishnu, can be found in the earliest portions of the Vedic literature. Here, he is known as Rudra (the "Howler"), and, again like Vishnu, he appears as one of many gods, or as one aspect of the overarching "Brahman," the spiritual essence of the universe. In the Vedas, he is god of the storms, accompanied by the Maruts, or the gods of destruction. These images of storm and destruction anticipate his later Hindu role as the demigod in charge of universal devastation.

The imposing form of Shiva is both heroic and awe-inspiring. He is usually depicted as whitish or ash-colored, with a blue-green neck (from holding in his throat a deadly poison produced during the churning of the cosmic ocean, a feat that is said to have occurred at the dawn of creation). His hair is often arranged in a spiral of matted locks, embellished with a crescent moon, a symbol of the Ganges River itself. It is said that he mysti-

Lord Shiva: When God manifests for cosmic destruction, he takes the form of this meditating ascetic. ©
2003 Mandala Publishing, www.mandala.org.

cally brought the river to the earth through his hair. Although he is often
depicted with two eyes, like most created beings, he is said to have a confidential third, which is sometimes visible in the middle of his forehead.
With this additional eye, he bestows inner vision on his devotees and burns
the universe to ashes when it is time for cosmic devastation. Shiva is also
known for the garland of skulls and hideous serpent wrapped around his
neck, as well as for the symbols found in his two (or sometimes four) hands:
a deerskin, a trident, a small hand-drum, and a club with a skull at the
end.

Shiva usually manifests in his own form; he does not come as multifarious incarnations (*avataras*). This is a distinction reserved for Vishnu. The
reasons for this distinction are many, although it can be explained in terms
of the essential nature of each deity. Vishnu is known for his benevolence,
and so he incarnates to help the fallen souls of the material world. Shiva, on
the other hand, is the unattached yogi. He is uninterested as to whether or
not one worships him. He has his own concerns, his own agenda.

Shiva as Nataraja: His dance of cosmic destruction is among Hinduism's most powerful visual images. © Corbis.

In terms of sculpture and painting, Shiva is depicted in a variety of forms:

1. He is represented in a calming, paternal mood, often with his wife Parvati, the Goddess discussed in the next section, and his sons, Skanda (also known as Karttikeya or Murugan) and Ganesh, the latter of whom is the famous elephant-headed lord of obstacles.
2. Shiva is also viewed as the cosmic dancer (Nataraja), whose dance brings each world cycle to an end; it is the exotic dance of universal destruction.
3. He is also commonly depicted as a naked ascetic, as the superlative renunciant, or as the consummate yogi, three ideals that are central to most forms of Shaivism.
4. Another prevalent portrayal of Shiva includes his androgynous form, which is basically a commingled union of him and his wife in one body, half-male and half-female.

Like Vishnu, he is known by many names and has many manifestations. Some of his more well-known epithets are Shambhu ("The Benevolent

One"), Shankara ("the Kind One"), Pashupati ("Lord of Beasts," or "Lord of Living Beings"), Maheshvara ("the Supreme Controller"), Mahadeva ("the Great God"), Rudra, and so on. Many of these names are also names of Vishnu, and, according to most Hindus, the overlapping of nomenclature is indicative of the underlying oneness between the gods. Vaishnavas aver that all reference to the divine is in fact a veiled reference to Vishnu, and it is for this reason that the names of the many gods are also appropriate for him.

The Major Schools of Shaivism

Major theological branches of Shaivism include the Pashupatas, Shaiva Siddhanta, Vira Shaivism, and Kashmir Shaivism, among others. Some of the characteristics of these groups are discussed here. The *Pashupatas* are generally considered the earliest sect of Shaivism, founded by Shiva himself, although the group was not a formalized tradition until well into the Common Era. This branch was largely an ascetic lineage established for monks, and their most important scripture, known as the Pashupata Sutra, was written by a sage named Lakulisha (ca. 100–200 C.E.). Lakulisha's commentator, Kaundinya, authored an explanatory text called the Panchartha Bhashya (400–600 C.E.). These are the two main scriptures studied by practitioners today.

The tradition has roots in the ancient world, when it was practiced in greater numbers, but adherents can still be found in various pockets of the subcontinent, particularly in Gujarat. Theologically, the Pashupatas accept the idea of a Supreme controller, or God, but they do not base their perceptions entirely on the Vedas, or India's most ancient holy books. Rather, they establish the existence of the Supreme on the basis of logic, and they conclude that Lord Shiva best embodies what God, as the Supreme Being, must be. However, they say that he alone is not the original cause of the material world. He is the operative cause in that he used already existing material ingredients. Thus, the world was created by a combination of his potency and that of the material energy, generally regarded as Shakti or Mother Durga (the wife of Lord Shiva).

The Pashupatas also gave rise to the controversial Kapalikas ("Skull Bearers") and the Kalamukhas ("Black-faced"), monks with dark practices, who traditionally cover their entire bodies with ash; have long, usually dirty, matted hair; and wear few if any clothes. They are generally quite austere, accomplished in various forms of yoga, and are otherwise given to eccentric practices. They are the most visible of wandering ascetics found at big festivals and celebrations, such as the Kumbha Mela.

Moving to alternate forms of Shaivism, *Shaiva Siddhanta* is also considered among the oldest branches of the tradition, and it is the most extensively practiced Shaiva denomination today, with millions of devotees, thousands of active temples, and numerous monastic traditions. This particular form of Shaivism originates and is largely practiced in South India. Philosophically, it is much akin to Vaishnavism (with Shiva replacing Vishnu, of course), and it has even been analyzed as a school of thought midway between impersonalism, which posits that God is essentially formless, and the Sri Vaishnava school of Qualified Monism, which acknowledges God's supreme form. That is to say, Shaiva Siddhanta supports the idea that God has both impersonal and personal features.

Its literature largely comprises the Shvetashvatara Upanishad; several Puranas, ancient books dedicated to Lord Shiva; 28 Shaivite Agamas, or scriptures that elucidate ritual performances in honor of Lord Shiva; the collection of Shaivite hymns known as Tirumurai, which was compiled by a devotee named Nambi Andar Nambi; the Periya Purana, a collection of short biographical sketches about Shaivite saints; and several other important South Indian works. This body of religious literature basically teaches that Shiva is the Supreme Godhead, and that the individual soul, in its perfected state, is in some sense the same as Shiva, although not identical to him. Shiva is great, say the Shaivites, but his devotees are small, like an ocean and the drops of water of which it is composed.

The Shaivite devotional movement, epitomized by Shaiva Siddhanta, had its greatest influence in South India between the seventh and eleventh centuries. This was roughly the same time that the mysticism of the Alvars, Vaishnava saints (emphasizing Vishnu as the Supreme Godhead), came to the fore. The devotees of Shiva at this time were known as Nayanars; they were like a Shaivite counterpart to the Alvars. Consequently, devotees from these two sides of the Hindu spectrum composed numerous hymns to Vishnu and Shiva, creating a particularly God consciousness environment throughout the south, eventually moving its way to the north. The inspiration fostered by this spiritual renaissance is felt even today, especially in the well-known temple areas of Tamilnadu. Here, Shaiva Siddhanta exists on a par with Vaishnavism, boasting an elaborate philosophical system of thought, lush temple worship, colorful festivals, creative arts, spiritual music, developed priestly procedures, and sophisticated educational institutions, social structures, and guru-disciple relationships.

Another significant Shaiva movement is *Vira Shaivism*, whose adherents are known as Vira Shaivas, or, alternatively, Lingayats. This important branch of Hinduism represents a reform movement originally attributed to a Shaivite holy man named Basavanna (1105–1167), who lived in Karnataka State (South India). Like Shaiva Siddhanta, the Lingayat movement is sometimes referred to as a form of "Shiva Vishishtadvaita," accepting both oneness and difference between the soul and God. In this sense, it is very much like Vaishnavism and even uses the same analogy for understanding humankind's relationship to God: The traditional analogy is that of the sun and sunshine, which are both one and different at the same time. The sunshine emanates from the sun, carrying its potency of heat and light, and in this way, where there is sun, there is sunshine. They are one. And, yet, the sunshine does not embody the full power of the sun. So they are different as well. Similarly, living beings come from God and reflect His potency, but they do not have that potency in full.

The Lingayats are thus essentially monotheistic in the sense that they view Shiva as the Supreme Deity, without considering the other Vedic gods as his competitors in any way. Lingayats strive for union and identity with Shiva—this is their clearly stated goal—which is more characteristic of monism, or the desire for oneness with God, than monotheism, or the living being's worship of a God that is totally Other. In this sense, they are very much unlike their Vaishnava counterparts. According to Lingayat philosophy, one merges with Shiva by a progressive six-stage path of devotion and surrender: initial faith, selfless service, taking grace, seeing Shiva in everything, acknowledging refuge in Shiva, and, ultimately, learning to feel complete oneness with Shiva. Each phase is explained in great detail, with procedures to guarantee gradual advancement. With each step one gets closer and closer to God, until the soul and its Maker coalesce in a perfected state of "Shiva consciousness," just in the same way that "a river might merge into the ocean."

An important feature of this group is its peculiar veneration of Shiva *lingam*—a phallic statue of the Deity's erect penis.[13] This *lingam* manifests as a small aniconic image, usually made of marble or stone, that is worshiped in temples and homes, instilling in its worshippers a sense of power and distinction. Interestingly, the word *lingam* is derived from the two Sanskrit roots, *laya* ("dissolution") and *agaman* ("re-creation"). Thus, Shiva *lingam*, in a higher sense, represents the Supreme entity who is in charge of cosmic creation and dissolution. In other words, the *lingam* symbolizes both the creative and destructive power of the universe, and the god who is at its helm—Lord Shiva.

Lingayats often wear the *lingam* around their necks so that worship can occur at any time of day, whenever inspiration arises, although it is usually reserved for certain regulated intervals. Unlike most religious Hindus, Lingayats deemphasize the Vedas, focusing instead more on the Agamas, or sectarian ritual texts.

Early adherents of the Lingayat religion attempted to rid society of caste distinctions, as was the case in many Vaishnava movements. Still, as in all Hindu branches, some sense of caste remains, expressed in greater or lesser degrees. In addition, Lingayats support equality between the genders, and therefore they not only have the usual male teachers, or gurus, but women gurus as well. This is found in Vaishnava traditions, too. Apparently, the devotional movements, whether Shaiva or Vaishnava, that swept the Indian subcontinent in medieval times were egalitarian in many modern and postmodern ways, making the age-old theistic traditions more appealing in an ever-changing world.

Kashmir Shaivism is yet another ancient branch of Shaivism, although it was not systematized until a vastly learned monk named Vasugupta, in as late as the ninth century, saw the need to do so. This form of Shaivism is clearly monistic; that is, it emphasizes the oneness of all that is, saying that all is Shiva, and that Shiva is all. Founded in Kashmir, in the far north, it grew into a thriving practice in the midst of controversial, heterodox traditions, such as Buddhism, the nontheistic discipline associated with the teachings of Siddhartha Gautama, and Tantric Shaktism, or the erotic worship of the Goddess.

According to the internal history of Kashmir Shaivism, Lord Shiva originally espoused 64 philosophical systems, ranging from deeply theistic traditions, acknowledging humankind's relationship with God, to monistic ideas of reality, claiming that all facets of existence—gods, humans, animals, nature, and so on—are ultimately one. But these systems of philosophy were eventually lost. Nonetheless, the founding fathers of Kashmir Shaivism were to lay a new foundation based on these ancient ideas, unearthing them by realization and closeness to God.

More than any other Shaiva tradition, Kashmir Shaivism is intensely monistic. This is not to say that it denies the existence of a personal God, but its emphasis is clearly on the individual soul and her own inherent divinity. The creation of the soul, in fact, is explained as Shiva's "shining forth," as his expanding of himself into all that is. Here, Shiva is both immanent and transcendent: He exists in the world as all living beings, and as material nature. He also exists in his kingdom in his spiritual form. Consequently, practitioners of Kashmir Shaivism are not interested in worshiping God as such, for, they reason, why should one worship an external God when one *is* God? Rather, Kashmir Shaivites spend their time in meditation and discipline, cultivating profound awareness of their own inner "Shiva Nature."

This is similar to another Shaivite path known as Shiva Advaita, which is also intensely monistic. However, this tradition was not always so. Conceived by Shrikantha (ca. 1050 C.E.), a Shaivite monk with Vaishnava leanings, Shiva Advaita originally opined that the soul does not ultimately become one with Shiva, or God. Rather, the soul shares all wonderful qualities with God while remaining distinct from Him. Like the Lingayats, this group was initially a form of Shiva Vishishtadvaita, claiming that the living being was both one with and yet different from God.

This early form of Shiva Advaita is thus similar to Vaishnavism, as are many other early Shaivite traditions, although here, naturally, Shiva displaces Vishnu. Still, if the gods are seen as being in some sense One, then these religious branches are actually diverse expressions of the same Truth. This is important to bear in mind, as most Hindus today tend to view the disparate Hindu traditions as alternate expressions of one overarching reality.

The philosophy of Shiva Advaita, however, eventually sprouted in a different direction, culminating in the appearance of Appaya Dikshita (1554–1626), a wandering ascetic of the Shaivite tradition. It was he, among others, who systematically argued for the absolute identity with the Deity. The actual goal of religion, he taught, is to become one with God. This follows in the tradition of Shankara (c. eighth century), who popularized oneness with God as a pan-Indian philosophical mindset. Such "oneness," however, is considered an offensive philosophy in most forms of Vaishnavism, and in the more monotheistic forms of Shaivism as well. These latter philosophical systems, Vaishnavas and Shaivas, argue that it is distasteful to want to end one's personal existence by merging with the Supreme and to thereby end God's personal existence as well. If one really loves God, they argue, one would want to go on being *separate* from Him, for only then can a loving relationship actually exist. Love, they say, requires lover and beloved, or the existence of two individuals, not one. As a Shaivite saint once put it, "I want to *taste* sugar, not *be* sugar."

There are many other branches of Shaivism. Some are monotheistic; others are not. Some look for a personal relationship with the Divine; others seek to realize their own inherent divinity. Overall, Shaivism promotes oneness with Shiva and the merging of one's consciousness with the Supreme Consciousness. This, says the Shaiva tradition, is the goal of life.

SHAKTISM: WORSHIP OF THE DIVINE MOTHER

The third major branch of modern Hinduism consists of worship of the Goddess, the divine feminine force of the universe, a religious sensibility that goes back to Vedic times and even earlier—giving it a history of at least 5,000 years. Most major forms of Hinduism, in fact, recognize both "male" and "female" dimensions of the Supreme, the only distinction being one of emphasis. In Vaishnavism and Shaivism, the Goddess is comparable to kinetic energy, in contradistinction to potential energy, which is found in the prominent deities, Vishnu and Shiva. In other words, the Goddess is seen as the burning power of fire, whereas Vishnu and Shiva are seen as fire itself. God is the energetic source, whereas the Goddess is the energy that flows from that source. In one sense, the energy and the energetic are one; in another, they are quite different.

Whereas certain Shakta or Goddess traditions also espouse this interrelationship of God and His energy, most forms of modern Shaktism break away from this theology of dependence. That is to say, they do not recognize any need for a "male" counterpart. They disavow any requirement for a greater entity from which or from whom the Goddess arises. Rather, she exists as the Supreme Entity, without relation to anyone else, or, alternatively, She is seen as the Deity's "better half" in that she has superior status in terms of her godhood. Indeed, Shiva's consort, known variously as Parvati, Durga, or Kali—or by a host of other names—is worshipped in most Shakta traditions as Supreme. She is, in fact, often depicted as trampling Shiva's Divine body, showing her preeminent position in relation to the male deity.

DEVI: THE WIFE OF LORD SHIVA

The word *Devi* appears in a plethora of Hindu texts. It is a word that means "Goddess." Vaishnavas would say that the original Goddess is Lakshmi, the Goddess of Fortune. She is Vishnu's consort and the epitome of the personified spiritual energy. In her more intimate, internal feature, she manifests as Radha, the consort of Lord Krishna, and in this esoteric form she is worshiped within specific schools of Vaishnavism. Radha expands into the many cowherd girls of Braj, who are considered Lord Krishna's most intimate devotees, and further into Ramadevi, or the energy at the heart of the spiritual world. It is this energy that further expands into Yoga-Maya and Maha-Maya, or the creative and/or illusory energy of the material world. These two forms of Maya are explained more fully in this section.

In general Indic discourse, the word Devi, or goddess, clearly refers to Durga, the goddess of the material sphere. Accordingly, it also refers to Parvati, the wife of Lord Shiva, for she is a well-known form of Durga. It is said, in fact, that Durga has more than 64 different forms, with different names for each form. These forms are so many manifestations of the same Universal Goddess, although they all have different characteristics—different visible features, emotions, activities, and interactions with living beings—displaying diverse aspects of her Divine nature. The more popular manifestations include Kali, Uma, Sati, Bhadra, Katyayani, and so on. All are well-known Hindu images; all are related to Shiva in one way or another.

In general, the Goddess represents matter (*prakriti*), a word that is cognate with "mother." This terminology hints at both her identity with material nature and her nurturing quality as the ultimate source or "parent" of all living beings. Shiva, it might be remembered, is the god of destruction. This has little meaning without created (i.e., material) objects that are capable of being destroyed. Thus, his counterpart, Durga, is viewed as equipping him with the material world—with people and with nature—giving substance to his service as the destructive feature of the Godhead. The implicit meaning here is that God brings everything into existence, and, in the end, winds everything up with cosmic devastation. In fact, the material world—with its creation and destruction—is described as Devi-dhama, or the realm of the Goddess. The word *durga* also means "prison house" or "fort," indicating that the material world is like a prison from which it is hard to escape. It is here that her potency is felt in its most intense form.

The connection between material nature and Maya (alternatively, Maha-Maya, another name for the Goddess), or material illusion, is important. The spiritual realm is viewed as eternal, full of knowledge and bliss. The material realm, by contrast, is a temporary place of ignorance and misery. Here, all beings die, real knowledge is conspicuous by its absence, and suffering is caused by humankind's inevitable separation from the people and objects to whom, and to which, they grow attached. Why, it might be asked, would people come to the material world, when their original home, in the spiritual realm, is clearly preferable in various fundamental ways? The typical Hindu answer is that people come to this world to be imitation gods, for the one thing they do not have in the spiritual kingdom is ultimate godhood. Rather, in that supreme world, they are merely devotees, happily serving God in a mood of love and devotion. Happy though they are, they are subservient nonetheless. A small number of rebellious souls thus become dissatisfied with this position and desire to usurp God's supreme status. The result is that they must go to a place where they can live out their illusion of imitation Lordship.

For this reason, the material world is created and then inhabited by living beings. To facilitate humankind's illusion, the Lord manifests as Maya, enabling the defiant souls to forget divinity and to become engrossed in the chimera of everyday falseness. Interestingly, Maya has an alternate form in the spiritual realm, called Yoga-Maya, and there she facilitates seemingly ordinary interaction between God and devotee through the agency of a similar kind of illusion. The distinction between Maya and Yoga-Maya, however, should be clearly understood: Whereas the material variety of Maya brings one ever further from spiritual Truth, the spiritual variety enhances one's relationship with God. That is to say, intimacy with the Supreme would be inconceivable if one were fully aware of God's greatness. Therefore, Yoga-Maya forges a kind of mystification, allowing one to interact with God in ways approximating simple, everyday relationships, and with the sweetness of loving exchange, ultimately creating an otherwise impossible intimacy between God and devotee.

Maya's chief form is that of Durga, a Sanskrit word that is often defined as "invincible," or "one who is difficult to know." She is often envisioned as a beautiful woman, with 4, 8, 10, 18, or 20 hands, depending on exactly which of her forms is under discussion. Items in her hands vary, but can include a trident, bow, arrow, sword, dagger, shield, rosary, and wine cup. The trident is especially significant, for the three-pronged weapon is symbolic of the three constituents of material nature—goodness, passion, and ignorance—which bind all living beings to the material world.

Durga is also visualized as standing on a lotus or, more commonly, riding a lion, or perhaps a tiger. The lion represents power, if also the animal tendency of greed, the selfishness that sustains the material world. By fearlessly riding this lion, she indicates her ability to keep all such tendencies under control, and her desire to punish all who do not.

Her exploits are detailed in a medieval book called the Devi Bhagavata, which is a popular text in the contemporary Hindu world, especially among worshippers of the Goddess. Such devotees also emphasize a scripture called the Durga Saptashati, which is a section of the Markandeya Purana, one of India's traditional sacred texts.

In these scriptures, Durga is described in many forms, and chief among them is "the Killer of the Buffalo Demon." In this form she is often pictured with 8 arms, sometimes 10, each with a weapon. Here she is glorified for

Queen Durga, the Goddess of the material world. She
rides atop her tiger carrier, ready to chastise all who
are evil. © 2003 Mandala Publishing, www.mandala.
org.

her killing of the demon Mahishasura, who is a tyrant in the guise of a buffalo. Briefly, the story runs as follows. Divinities such as Vishnu, Shiva, and
Brahma were vexed by this buffalo demon and his army, for by their nefari-
ous deeds they were ruining the earth. Thus, the Indic Trinity, as a product
of their vexation, called forth the beautiful Goddess to slay the demon.

Atop her fierce lion, she mystically appeared in full adulthood. She
fought and killed Mahishasura and his accompanying troops. This defeat is
significant. The demon and his associates represent egoism, brute strength,
and selfish desires, while the Goddess represents the softer characteristics
needed to conquer such demons. It is also said that the buffalo demon can
be identified with laziness, ignorance, and inertia, and that it takes the subtlety of a more feminine spirituality to defeat such demons. In this sense,
the Devi is sometimes seen as a warrior goddess, who slashes our more
subtle enemies.

The idea is that the gentleness of true God (or Goddess) consciousness
destroys the lower nature within each of us, for, without submission to the
Supreme, these subtle materialistic problems can be difficult to overcome.

While fighting against Vishnu, Shiva, and Brahma, Mahishasura was suc-
ceeding until their combined powers and their will to protect the world
was manifest as the Devi, as "the Killer of the Buffalo Demon." Hindus
who favor the Goddess often find in this a justification for the worship of a
feminine divinity as opposed to that of a masculine one. Still, all forms of
Hindu spirituality take this into consideration, and therefore there is always
a dual—female and male—divinity: Radha-Krishna, Lakshmi-Vishnu, Sita-
Rama, and Durga-Shiva. If most forms of Hinduism tend to emphasize the
male aspect of the divine, Shaktas emphasize the female aspect.

From the forehead of Durga manifests the fierce, dark Kali ("the black
one"), a particularly fearsome expression of the Goddess specifically meant
for killing demons. Kali is the ultimate Hindu mother goddess, and yet she is
a symbol of rage and destruction as well. Ultimately, however, she destroys
ignorance, and by so doing maintains worldly order. In the Vedas, India's
most ancient sacred texts, the name Kali is associated with Agni, the god of
fire, who was known for his seven tongues of flame, of which Kali was the
black, hideous tongue. This frightful imagery has stayed with the Goddess
in later literature. In fact, her appearance is the most fearsome of any major
divinity: She has menacing eyes, a protruding tongue, four arms ready for
the kill, and a general demeanor of horror. She is often depicted as running
about without any clothes, and her form is the stuff of nightmares.

In her upper left hand she holds a bloody sword and, in her lower left,
the severed head of a demon, with drops of blood dripping to the ground.
With her upper right hand she shows the gesture of fearlessness; with the
lower one she offers rewards to her devotees. A garland of severed human
heads is draped around her neck, and she wears a belt composed of dismembered arms. As the Divine Mother, she is depicted as dancing, or,
sometimes, in loving embrace with Shiva, her husband. As the redeemer
of the universe, she is visualized as standing on him, Shiva, who is reclining
in corpselike fashion, caught beneath her feet. She is variously known as
Kalikamata ("black earth-mother") and, in southern India, as Kottavei. She
is worshipped particularly in Bengal, where her most famous temples are
in Kalighat and Dakshineshvara.[14]

There is much symbolic meaning in her frightful form. Ultimately, Kali
represents time, Kala, which devours everything in due course. She often
holds a snake, which also signifies the destructive principle of time. This
frightful truth of each person's ultimate defeat at the hands of time is at
the heart of Kali's image. She is sometimes depicted as naked because she
is free from the opaque veil of ignorance, which covers most people until
the time they die. Her nakedness also represents her lack of misconcep-

tion, a misconception that tends to clothe humankind throughout their so-journ in innumerable species. Her blackness, both in color and demeanor, represents the mode of darkness—the incalculable ignorance that engulfs all people—and the deep well of material existence, into which all created things must one day fall. Her apron of dismembered hands and arms indicates both that she is pleased with the offerings of her devotees and that she is willing to cut off the arms of those who act sinfully.

Animal sacrifices are not uncommon in Kali worship. This is perhaps originally traced to ancient Vedic rituals or, some say, to Durga's killing of the buffalo demon; buffalo, in fact, are the animals usually offered to the Goddess today. During the 3-day annual autumn festival of Durga Puja, almost 1,000 male goats are slaughtered in her honor at Kalighat alone.[15] Such animal sacrifice, however, is on the wane. Those who are averse to it, and to meat eating in general, tend to offer red flowers instead of blood offerings. Still, the Goddess is well known for her bloodthirsty feature as Kali.

If Durga is Goddess as warrior, and Kali as bloodthirsty heroine, then Parvati is Goddess as Mother and nurturer of life. Parvati's story begins with her prior birth. According to Hindu tradition, Shiva was once married to an unusually dedicated young woman named Sati. One day, Daksha, Sati's father, neglected to invite Her, and, more important, Her famed husband, Shiva, to an important Vedic sacrifice. Showing intense indignation for her father's insolence, She tragically committed suicide by setting herself on fire.[16] When Shiva discovered what had happened, he could not contain himself. Inconsolable, the distraught widower vowed never to marry again.

Still, years later, a young women named Parvati ("Daughter of the Mountain") committed herself to an austere life of meditation, just to win him as her husband. She meditated in the Himalayas for years (hence her name) without shelter or home, unswerving in her determination even in the midst of torrential rains, blistering heat, and other natural calamities. One day, she heard a child cry, and, because of maternal instinct, she immediately broke her meditation, desiring to lend a helping hand. Much to her surprise, the child's cry had actually come from Shiva, who was merely testing her resolve. She had failed the test, but Shiva was so moved by the fact that she would give up what she desired most to help someone in need, that he took her as his wife. The teaching here is clear: There are "heart" considerations that are more important than vows and predetermined austerities.

As the mother of the universe, Parvati is known as Amba and Ambika, which literally means "mother." Hindu tradition teaches that Shiva and Parvati had two children: the elephant-headed Ganesh and the warrior, Skanda, representing success and beauty. These two are glorified throughout the subcontinent, particularly in South India, where Skanda is more commonly known as Murugan or Karttikeya, and Ganesh as Ganapati. As the supernatural sons of Shiva and Parvati, they are frequently seen as gods in themselves and are often worshipped independently of their divine parents.

SHAKTISM IN PRACTICE

The original ideas of the Shakta belief system, like those of Vaishnavism and Shaivism, can be traced back to the Rig Veda and other Vedic and post-Vedic works. Of course, like the other traditions, Shaktism is not explicitly outlined in these earliest texts, nor does the specific theology come to the fore until many centuries later. When it finally did, in the fifth or seventh century, the Shaktas evolved into two groups: one called the Right-Hand, and the other, the Left-Hand. The Right-Hand is an ascetic group, but its practices are not controversial; and, in many respects, it is very much like other Hindu groups today. The Left-Hand, by contrast, is a group that combines yogic exercises with practices that break the boundaries of orthodoxy. These "outside" practices are called the *Panchamakara*, or the five Ms of Shaktism. These are *Madya* (wine), *Mamsa* (meat), *Matsya* (fish), *Mudra* (parched grain, or aphrodisiac cereals), and *Maithuna* (ritual sex). Usually shunned in other Hindu branches, the drinking of wine, the eating of meat and fish, and certain prescribed sexual activities are here used as part of a sacrificial rite, incorporating intoxicating parched grain; these are the special accoutrements in the particular worship of Kali or Durga.

Shaktism has intimate connections with Tantra, a word usually identified with religiously ordained sexual practices or magical formulas that serve to satisfy bodily appetites. Originally, Tantra referred to certain ritual texts and practices that involve yoga and worship, or strict adherence to penance and austerity for a highly spiritual result. The ascetic process of the Tantric path is similar to Raja-yoga and Kundalini-yoga, both quite popular today. These yoga systems involve the evolution of spiritual energy, and the scientific method of raising this energy through various portals of the body, resulting in the elevation of one's consciousness. Through sitting postures, breathing exercises, and meditation techniques, the practitioner seeks to raise his or her consciousness and free the soul from material entanglement. The Goddess, being the supreme energy incarnate, both helps the practitioner raise the energy in the body and, in a sense, *is* this self-same energy. Thus, the Goddess is central to the whole yogic process associated with Shaktism and Tantric practice.

Ultimately, most forms of Shaktism, like Shaivism, are monistic, encouraging "oneness" with the Goddess, although there is a sense of devotion to the Divine Mother. The goal is *moksha*, or liberation, usually conceived as merging with the spiritual energy of the universe, or, alternatively, with Shiva through the agency of this energy. Indeed, as many Vaishnavas worship Radha or Laksmi as a Divine Mediatrix, so, too, do many Shaktas worship the Goddess as a means to Shiva. In this sense, Shaktism is sometimes viewed as a subdivision of Shaivism. Overall, however, it is an independent tradition of devotion to the feminine energy, the ultimate Goddess, and many devotees in the subcontinent develop love for the divine in this way.

THE THREE MAJOR BRANCHES TODAY

There are other branches of Hinduism such as the worship of the sun; veneration of Hanuman, the monkey-god; or offering homage to Ganesh, the elephant-headed son of Lord Shiva. There is also Smartism, wherein India's many gods are all honored as distinct deities. Nonetheless, Vaishnavism, Shaivism, and Shaktism, and their offshoots, clearly dominate Hinduism's religious landscape.

Although Buddhism, Jainism, and Sikhism, as Indic religions, are not forms of "Hinduism" as such, they are often lumped in as revisionist Hindu traditions, as remote branches within the Hindu complex of religions. Buddhism refers to the tradition founded by Siddhartha Gautama, "the Buddha," a sage from about 500 B.C.E., who taught various techniques of psychological empowerment and fundamental truths of existence. Jainism, a similar nontheistic tradition that emphasizes "harmlessness," or *ahimsa* was systematized by Mahavira, another sage who flourished during the time of the Buddha. And Sikhism, a tradition founded by Guru Nanak in the sixteenth century, is an interesting blend of Hindu and Islamic doctrine. These three traditions do not trace their theology to the Vedas and are thus considered Hindu heterodoxies, if Hindu at all. There *are* those who would include these religions within the jurisdiction of Hinduism, as in, for example, the Orissa Religious Endowments Act of 1969, giving the inclusion of these groups a legal backdrop. This Act is still in effect and states that "the expression 'Hindu religion' shall include Jain, Buddhist, and Sikh religions, and the expressions 'Hindu' and 'Hindu public religious institutions and endowments' shall be construed accordingly." Such laws, in tandem with the egalitarian nature of contemporary Hindu pluralism, allow the three heterodox religions mentioned here to be viewed as branches of Hinduism.

The three overarching branches—Vaishnavism, Shaivism, and Shaktism—constitute the main substance of the Hindu tree of knowledge. These three have many representatives in the world today, sprouting into metaphorical twigs, flowers, and numerous fruits. Three examples follow: a modern Vaishnava movement, a modern Shaiva movement, and a modern Shakta movement, although there are many others as well. The Swaminarayana religion, for example, is one of many modern Vaishnava movements; the Siddha Yoga Dham people are descended from Kashmir Shaivism (with elements of Shaktism as well); and the Adi Para Sakti movement in southern India is a well-known Shakta tradition.

THE HARE KRISHNA MOVEMENT

The International Society for Krishna Consciousness (ISKCON), also known as "the Hare Krishnas," a modern-day Vaishnava movement, has roots in the ancient Brahma-Madhva-Sampradaya. That is, it has a distinct connection to the esoteric lineage beginning with Brahma, the creator-god, in prehistory. It can be traced through the great religious reformer, Madhva, into medieval times, it blossomed in sixteenth-century India with the arrival of Sri Chaitanya, the ecstatic incarnation of Krishna who revolutionized Hindu spirituality with his emphasis on devotional love and on the nonsectarian chanting of God's holy names. Sri Chaitanya taught that devotional love and spiritual chanting were the most effective religious practices in the contemporary world. Chaitanya's Vaishnavism is strictly monotheistic, with a clear separation between God and the living entity, whose constitutional position consists of serving the Supreme.

In 1965, at the age of 70, His Divine Grace A. C. Bhaktivedanta Swami Prabhupada (1896–1977), born Abhay Charan De, convinced a wealthy supporter who owned a steamship company to pay his passage to the United States. His desire to go abroad was in pursuance of an order from his spiritual preceptor, Srila Bhaktisiddhanta Sarasvati Thakur (1874–1937), who claimed that it was time for the universal teaching at the heart of their Vaishnava tradition to be carried around the world.

Prabhupada had spent a lifetime in preparation for this, although it is unlikely that he was aware of it. He had studied English, economics, and philosophy at Scottish Churches' College in Calcutta, which prepared him for communicating with a Western audience, managing a worldwide movement, and explaining Vaishnavism to potential devotees coming from different philosophical backgrounds, respectively. While still in India, he had translated several Vaishnava classics and even initiated a monthly periodi-cal, *Back to Godhead* magazine, in 1944—and it still enjoys a worldwide circulation.

On the surface, it appeared that Prabhupada came to the United States equipped only with his own partial translation of the Shrimad Bhagavatam (one of India's ancient scriptures), a few rupees, and the clothing on his back. However, he actually came with the teachings of an age-old lineage, the blessings of the great teachers in that line, and quite a bit of personal experience. His learning and devotion were indomitable, and his integrity as a renounced holy person was also unassailable.

Once he arrived, he settled briefly New York's Lower East Side, where he held the first outdoor chanting sessions in Tompkins Square Park. Young hippies and intellectuals began to flock to him, attracted as much to the "Eastern mysticism" of Krishna consciousness as to Prabhupada's personal charisma. In July 1966, he formally established ISKCON in New York City, and centers quickly opened around the world.

His Divine Grace A. C. Bhaktivedanta Swami Prab-hupada (1896–1977), in constant meditation on his worshipable Radha and Krishna. © 2003 Mandala Publishing, www.mandala.org.

The group's central teachings focus on the chanting of Krishna's names ("Hare Krishna, Hare Krishna, Krishna Krishna, Hare Hare/ Hare Rama, Hare Rama, Rama Rama, Hare Hare"). The prayer is translated as follows: "O Lord! O Energy of the Lord [Mother Hara, or Radha]! Please engage me in Lord Krishna's service." Chanting this prayer allows one to develop an intimate relationship with Krishna by direct association (because God and His name are nondifferent). Devotees chant softly on rosary beads, as a personal meditation; they chant congregationally, which includes singing the prayer (and others) in various melodies; and they take congregational chanting into the street as well, to help the masses by giving them easy access to the holy name.

Also central to Hare Krishna practice is *prasadam* distribution, which is the free dispersal of sacred vegetarian food, believed to purify all who eat it, although this same food is also sold in their many successful restaurants. In addition to *prasadam* there is book distribution, a practice that is considered especially sacred in its attempt to spread Krishna's teachings to all who will listen. Personal austerities include refraining from meat, fish, or eggs and a ban on illicit sex or sex outside of marriage, intoxication, and gambling. Devotees also rise early for congregational services in which Krishna is glorified with song and dance, personal meditations, and scriptural readings.

There are hundreds of ISKCON temples in every inhabited continent and in most countries throughout the world. In North America alone, there are 60 temples and/or rural communities and restaurants. In India, where the movement is especially successful and recognized as a valid religious tradition, it is flourishing more than ever before. ISKCON has had its share of problems, however, with post-Prabhupada leaders defecting, splinter groups being created, and membership dwindling in certain regions. Still, great success stories continue to form on the back page of ISKCON's history: Food For Life (in which ISKCON members feed the hungry throughout the world) and other altruistic initiatives are growing rapidly, and Prabhupada's books continue to appear in a multitude of languages. Devotees learn from their mistakes, and fanaticism is slowly being replaced with education and the benefits of experiential knowledge.

In short, ISKCON has indeed carried on throughout the world after Prabhupada's demise, although with great difficulty. The founder remains the movement's beacon light. The *1976 Britannica Book of the Year* stated that "he astonished academic and literary communities worldwide by writing and publishing fifty-two books on the ancient Vedic culture ... in the

Hare Krishna devotee. © Getty Images/2100005693.

period from October 1968 to November 1975." Add to this that in his old age, he had circled the globe 14 times, lecturing, corresponding with dignitaries, friends and disciples, and overseeing the opening of temples, restaurants, and farm communities. His scholarship, devotional demeanor, and diligence in training disciples only grew with the years. Clearly, in Prabhupada's life, historians have the stuff of legends.[17]

SHAIVA SIDDHANTA CHURCH

The Shaiva Siddhanta Church, often known as "the Hinduism Today" people, is a spiritual institution dedicated to promoting the Shaivite religion in the modern world. It has ancient roots in both the Nandinatha Sampradaya and the Kailasha Parampara, both recognized Shaivite lineages. It appeals to pan-Indian consciousness by including all Hindu traditions, much like the Smartas of India, who see all the gods as one, although here Shaivism is necessarily emphasized. It also appeals to today's youth by making use of modern media and other accoutrements of modernity.

The Church was the brainchild of Satguru Shivaya Subramuniyaswami (1927–2001), a white-haired renunciant of Nordic descent. Officially, he founded the Church in 1949, but it was not formally incorporated until 1957. Among his followers, he was affectionately known as Gurudeva. Born Robert Walter Hansen in Oakland, California, he rose to become one of the most prominent figures in Hinduism during the 1980s and 1990s.

As a youth, he was trained in classical dance and in various yoga traditions. Excelling at both, he became the premier dancer of the San Francisco Ballet by age 19. His interest in yoga, however, soon took over, and he renounced the world in search of the Absolute. His search took him to India, and then, in 1948, deep into the jungles of Sri Lanka, in the caves of Jalani, where he underwent severe austerities, fasting and meditating. At this time, it is said, he reached a profound level of realization. After this, his reputation as a saintly person spread far and wide, and, as a result, he eventually met his eternal teacher, Sage Yogaswami (1872–1964), who initiated him as a monk in the Shaivaite lineage for which he is now famous.

Subramuniyaswami's well-worn phrases, "Know thyself by thyself" and "Try to see Shiva everywhere," are fundamental to the group's teachings, which are essentially monistic; that is, in the ultimate analysis, everything is Shiva and Shiva is everything. Such enlightenment is accomplished, Subramuniyaswami taught, through self-inquiry, meditation, temple worship,

Satguru Shivaya Subramuniyaswami (1927–2001), leader and inspiration of the Shaiva Siddhanta Church. © 2003 Mandala Publishing, www.mandala.org.

selfless service, and the study of the scriptures, which are indeed the activities his movement promotes.

For more than 50 years, his Shaiva Siddhanta Church has produced a plethora of dedicated "swamis"—a monastic order that seeks to help the world in numerous ways. In pursuance of this mandate, they have established a theological seminary to train religious leaders. In addition, the movement offers the world a number of important services: More than a quarter of a million readers, a conservative estimate if one considers those accessing it on the Internet, now subscribe to their award-winning monthly journal, *Hinduism Today*, founded in 1979. It started out as a humble newspaper but, in 1996, was upgraded to a glossy magazine. The group has published numerous books as well, detailing what it means to be a Hindu generally, and a Shaivite in particular.

They have worked hard to promote the use of sophisticated Hindu graphics, arranging for free public use. They also make it a point to patronize all forms of Hindu-related art, which is one of their many attempts to broadcast the richness of Indian culture. They have opened schools for children and emphasized the importance of Hindu sacraments, such as namegiving, first-feeding, marriage, and funeral rites. This has been an especially valuable service for Hindus living outside India. Conscious of traditional concerns in this regard, all of these endeavors were embarked on with the aid of an advisory council composed of priests, scholars, swamis, and other respected leaders in India and Sri Lanka, as well as those in the United States, Mauritius, Malaysia, Europe, and South Africa.

The Church's international headquarters is Kauai's Hindu Monastery, Kauai Aadheenam, located on the Hawaiian island although there are now other centers with local missions in more than eight countries. The ordained monks at these centers receive no remuneration, and they give of themselves voluntarily. They arise before dawn to engage in a disciplined but joyous life of worship, meditation, and altruistic service, engaging steadfastly in the ancient traditions of Shaivite monasticism, including vows of purity, humility, and obedience. Those who are "swamis," or the highest-ranking monks, in particular, must adhere to the vow of lifetime renunciation.[18]

On August 25, 2000, approximately 1 year before he passed away, Subramuniyaswami received the distinguished U Thant Peace Award at the United Nations (which had previously been granted to such luminaries as the Dalai Lama, Nelson Mandela, Pope John Paul II, and Mother Teresa) in New York City. When he returned to Kauai, dozens of politicians and hundreds of citizens gathered to glorify his accomplishments on the island and around the world. Governor Benjamin Cayetano wrote: "I am especially grateful for your efforts to promote moral and spiritual values in Hawaii. May our people forever embrace the message of peace you have so eloquently supported in your gracious wisdom." He will be missed by all practitioners of Hinduism, even though his mission certainly lives on.

THE RAMAKRISHNA MISSION

The Ramakrishna Mission, based on the teachings of the Indian mystic known as Ramakrishna (1836–1886), born Gadadhar Chatterjee, is a pan-Hindu religious institution that is primarily dedicated to the worship of the Goddess. It is therefore often seen as a Shakta movement, although there is some controversy regarding this categorization, which is discussed later. The Mission is a vast network of temples, schools, hospitals, and relief centers. With its headquarters at Belur, in Calcutta, the Mission has two main branches—one emphasizes religion and preaching and another specializes in welfare services of various kinds.

The religious segment of the Mission has 82 sub-branches, with 68 of them in India. The remaining 8 are in Bangladesh, and 1 each in Fiji, France, Mauritius, Singapore, Sri Lanka, and Switzerland. Others open periodically. The altruistic, welfare portion of the Mission has 77 branches, mostly in India but also in Canada, France, Japan, England, and the United States.

The entire Mission was founded by Swami Vivekananda (1863–1902), chief among Ramakrishna's disciples, whose birth name was Narendranath Datta. Having been the representative of Hinduism at the consequential Parliament of Religions conference in Chicago (in 1893), he conceived of the Mission on his return to India in 1897. Years later, in the late 1930s, his immediate followers, under the direction of Swami Prabhavananda, founded the Vedanta Society in California, which attracted such notables as Aldous Huxley and Christopher Isherwood, popular writers on Eastern mysticism. ("Vedanta" is a Sanskrit word meaning "the ultimate conclusion of knowledge," which is what the movement claims to have accessed.)

The Ramakrishna Mission is one of the earliest and largest Hindu organizations in the world. But are they Shaktas? It has been argued that Swami Vivekananda, the founder of the mission, took the teachings of a Shakta religious leader (Ramakrishna) and retooled them into a kind of generic Hinduism. This is true, but the Mission's centers in India (and also most of its branches in other Asian countries) celebrate the traditional and elab-

Swami Vivekananda (1863–1902), the organiza-
tional head of the Ramakrishna Mission. Courtesy
of the Ramakrishna Vedanta Society.

orate worship services of the Shakta tradition, emphasizing the specifics
and festivals associated with Durga, Kali, Lakshmi, and other forms of the
Goddess. Many of the centers in the West also observe the annual Durga
Puja and Kali Puja ceremonies, which are distinct among Shaktas, but in a
condensed format. The center in Southern California has an elaborate, all-
night Kali Puja, a celebration of the Goddess that highlights the Mission's
yearly activities in that part of the world.

In addition, many of the members and followers of the movement, both
monastic and lay people, consider the Goddess (in any of her various forms,
such as Kali, Durga, and so on) their "Chosen Deity," and this makes her
central to their personal meditation practice. At the heart of all this is the
visionary who is inspired the movement, Sri Ramakrishna, who is known as
the "Child of the Divine Mother." Monks and devotees of the Ramakrishna
Mission want to emulate their Master, feeling a certain eagerness to also
become children of the Divine Mother, by seeking her grace. They pray to

her earnestly: "O Great Goddess, You are all-pervasive, the Mother of all. We know, O Mother, that if You are pleased, everyone is pleased."

The Shakta worship of Ramakrishna, tending toward monism, or identity with the Divine, was brought to a new level by his wife, known as "the living Durga." Her name was Sri Sarada Devi (1853–1920), and she also worshipped the Divine Goddess, instructing others to do the same. Expressing the Motherhood of God in her own much-loved example, rendering selfless service to all with whom she came into contact, she added additional impetus to Ramakrishna's Shakta inclinations. In due course, however, the Ramakrishna Mission was created and evolved into an institution with more pragmatic concerns, with general spiritual principles and altruistic endeavors often superseding the abstract, or the religious.

The Ramakrishna Mission's 1994 report details their activities in India under the following six categories: (1) relief, (2) welfare, (3) medical, (4) education, (5) spread of spiritual and cultural ideas, and (6) projects in rural and tribal areas. Along with four basic concepts—(1) the oneness of existence, (2) the divinity of human beings; (3) the unity of God; and (4) the harmony of religions—all 10 sum up the activities of the Mission. The Mission is also summed up by Swami Vivekananda in the following way: "The Christian is not to become a Hindu or a Buddhist, nor a Hindu or a Buddhist to become a Christian. But each must assimilate the spirit of the others and yet preserve his own identity and grow according to his own law of growth. I hope that upon the banner of every religion will soon be written, in spite of resistance, 'help' and not 'fight,' 'assimilation' and not 'destruction,' 'harmony and peace' and not 'dissension.'"[19]

Ramakrishna himself is not considered the founder of the Ramakrishna Mission, or its later subsidiary, the Vedanta Society, because of his firm belief in not seeking out followers, although many definitely came to him. He did not see himself as a leader or as the founder of any particular organization. In fact, he rejected formalized creeds and singular paths to the Divine, seeing truth in all paths. Thus, the founding of the institution fell on the able shoulders of Swami Vivekananda, who not only organized the original Mission and brought Hinduism to the United States through the World's Parliament of Religions, as stated, but who was also the first Hindu to instigate Hinduism"s growth in the West. It could be argued, too, that Ramakrishna's vision of Hinduism, and its popularization by Western converts such as British author Christopher Isherwood (1906–1986) have largely shaded Western notions of what Hinduism actually is. Had Vaishnavas or Shaivites attended that momentous religious conference or preceded

Vivekananda in influencing Western converts, the world might now have a very different conception of the Hindu complex of religions.

NOTES

1. A.L. Basham, *The Wonder That Was India* (New York: Grove Press, 1954), p. 309.

2. See especially F.B.J. Kuiper, "The Three Strides of Visnu," in *Indological Studies in Honor of W. Norman Brown* (New Haven, CT: American Oriental Society, 1962), pp. 137–151. Here the uniqueness of Vishnu is elaborated on, as is his supremacy among the gods. See also Deborah A. Soifer, *The Myths of Narasimha and Vamana: Two Avatars in Cosmological Perspective* (Albany: State University of New York Press, 1991), p. 19, where, based on Vedic evidence, she writes, "Vishnu is clearly demonstrating a pervasive nature unparalleled by any other Vedic god."

3. "Vishnu is the sacrifice" is a Vedic aphorism. It can be found in the Kaushitaki Brahmana (4.2, 18.8, and 18.14), the Aitareya Brahmana (3.4), the Shatapatha Brahmana (1.9.3.9), and many others. The implications of this aphorism were not fully appreciated until the epics and the Puranas.

4. The dating of Vedic literature is always tentative. In terms of dating, in fact, the epics and the Puranas, especially, allow for a large margin of error. Some parts of this literature are clearly pre-Christian; other parts may be from as late as 800–900 C.E.

5. It is said that in the time of the Buddha, people were misinterpreting Vedic texts, using them to rationalize meat eating. Vaishnava sages say that the Buddha specifically came to put an end to such misunderstanding and hypocrisy. For more on Buddha as an incarnation of Vishnu, see the Bhagavata Purana (1.3.24) and the twelfth-century classic Jayadeva's Gita-Govinda. See also Steven J. Rosen, *From Nothingness to Personhood: A Collection of Essays on Buddhism from a Vaishnava-Hindu Perspective* (New York: FOLK Books, 2003).

6. This is the standard list of incarnations, although unlimited numbers of them are not mentioned here. The stories associated with these incarnations are here given in extremely abbreviated format. The scriptures expound on these divine manifestations in numerous ways, including details for each one that could constitute a book in itself.

7. The idea of Krishna's supremacy is clearly articulated in the Bhagavata Purana (1.3.28), cited here. There are, however, Vaishnava traditions that deemphasize this fact and those that obscure it altogether.

8. See A. L. Basham, *A Cultural History of India* (Oxford: Oxford University Press, 1975), p. 81.

9. Vaishnavism is a multifaceted religion that always centers on the worship of Vishnu. However, Vishnu has many incarnations and manifestations, such as Krishna or Rama, and a great many Vaishnavas focus instead on these particular forms of Vishnu. This is significant because, in several Vaishnava theological systems, Krishna is considered the original Godhead, the source of Vishnu. Hence, such traditions might more aptly be called forms of Krishnaism as opposed to Vaishnavism. The Gaudiya Vaishnavas and the Pushti-marg are two such theological systems, sub-branches of the greater Vaishnava heritage.

10. This summarization of Vaishnava doctrine is a loosely translated version of Bhaktivinoda Thakur's "Ten-Rooted Truth of Vaishnava Wisdom." For a more literal translation, see his *Gauranga-lila-smarana-stotram: Auspicious Meditations on Lord Gauranga,* trans., Kusakratha dasa (Los Angeles: The Krsna Institute, 1988), Verse 75. Various Vaishnava sects articulate their basic teachings in various ways, emphasizing one particular point mentioned in this list, or omitting another. Overall, however, Bhaktivinoda's summation should give the reader a basic idea about what Vaishnavas believe.

11. For more on the "cat and monkey disparity," see Patricia Y. Mumme, *The Srivaisnava Theological Dispute* (Madras: New Era Publications, 1988). See also Thomas A. Forsthoefel and Patricia Y. Mumme, "The Monkey-Cat Debate in Srivaisnavism" *Journal of Vaishnava Studies* 8 (1999). In this article, Pillai Lokacharya (1264–1369), another luminary of the Sri Vaishnava Tradition (and the teacher for whom Manavalama Muni was merely a literary commentator), is given credit for developing the "cat" dimension of the debate.

12. In the Brahma-samhita (5.45), an ancient Vaishnava text containing esoteric details about God's inner nature, Shiva is said to be another form of Vishnu: "Just as milk is transformed into curd by the actions of acids, but yet the effect of curd is neither the same as, nor different from, its cause, viz., milk, so I adore the primeval Lord Krishna (Vishnu) of whom the state of Shiva is a transformation for the performance of the work of destruction." In addition to this view of Shiva as a variation on Vishnu and thus a manifestation of God, the Bhagavata Purana (12.13.16) regards Shiva as Vishnu's greatest devotee.

13. The name *Vira Shaiva* is derived from *vira* ("heroic"), and *shaiva* ("worshipper of Shiva"), whereas *Lingayat* comes from the word *lingam,* or the abstract symbol of Shiva's genitalia, indicating his virile (*vira?*) nature. The earliest iconographic evidence of the *lingam* as a phallic symbol is the Gudimallam Lingam in Andhra Pradesh, dated at ca. 2nd century B.C.E. The phallic nature of the *lingam* is elaborated on in *Religions of India in Practice,*

ed. Donald Lopez, Jr. (Princeton, NJ: Princeton University Press, 1995) pp. 637–648.

14. The name *Calcutta* is an Anglicized version of the word *Kalighat*, which means "Kali Temple," indicating that Calcutta was the city of Kali. Even today, as stated, Hindus in Bengal, and especially in Calcutta, favor Kali worship.

15. Before human sacrifice was prohibited in 1835, male and female children were sometimes beheaded to appease Goddess Kali.

16. Some say this is the origin of the controversial act of *sati*, in which a widow throws herself on the funeral pyre of her recently departed husband, committing suicide. For more on *sati*, which has been illegal in most of India since 1829, see John S. Hawley's edited volume, *Sati: The Blessing and the Curse* (New York: Oxford University Press, 1994).

17. For more on the Hare Krishna movement, see Charles R. Brooks, *The Hare Krishnas in India* (Princeton, NJ: Princeton University Press, 1989), and David G. Bromley and Larry D. Shinn, eds., *Krishna Consciousness in the West* (Lewisburg, PA: Bucknell University Press, 1989). For an insider perspective, see Satsvarupa Dasa Goswami, *Srila Prabhupada-lilamrta*, 6 volumes (Los Angeles: The Bhaktivedanta Book Trust, 1980–1983).

18. For an overview of Shaiva Siddhanta, see the Shaiva Dharma Shastras, as well as other books published by the movement. For more on the Shaiva Siddhanta Church, see Satguru Sivaya Subramuniyaswami, *Living with Siva, Hinduism's Contemporary Culture* (Hawaii: Himalayan Academy, 2001).

19. For more on Ramakrishna and his mission, see *Life of Ramakrishna* (Calcutta: Advaita Ashrama, 1983, reprint). Also see Swami Nikhilananda, trans., *The Gospel of Sri Ramakrishna* (New York: The Ramakrishna-Vivekananda Center, 1984, reprint) and Jeffrey J. Kripal, *Kali's Child: The Mystical and the Erotic in the Life and Teachings of Ramakrishna* (Chicago: University of Chicago Press, 1995).

4

PRACTICE WORLDWIDE

There were three major incursions of Hinduism into the Western world and into other parts of Asia in recent history. These form a sort of backdrop against which worldwide Hindu practice can be understood. The first incursion occurred during the nineteenth and early twentieth centuries. Looking for employment and a better life, Indians immigrated to Burma, South Africa, the Fiji Islands, and the West Indies, among other places. By the 1920s, at least 2 million Indians, mainly Hindus, found themselves outside of India, usually in British colonies and dominions. These Hindu immigrants generally found themselves in impoverished conditions, usually working as indentured servants.[1] Still, they thought of this as a step up from life in a developing nation, although, in their new homes, they often lived in ethnic communities with little possibility for upward social or economic mobility.

Around this same time and soon thereafter, there was a second wave of "immigrants," but this time it was not composed of people. Hindu philosophy, in the form of translations of sacred texts and cultural treatises, from the Vedas to the Bhagavad Gita, made its appearance, often for the first time in non-Indian languages, outside India and quickly finding a home among intellectuals around the world. The "Mystic East" was popularized as the exotic land of the Upanishads, and dabblers included such luminaries as Emerson and Thoreau. This evolved into an interest by the Beat poets of the 1960s and the emergence of various "new religions" with a Hindu twist, from the Theosophical Movement, a Western tradition based on Eastern principles, to the International Society for Krishna Consciousness (see Chapter 3), some of which had ancient roots in India.

The third wave of Hindus to leave India was in some ways most important of all: While the second wave was gaining steam in the 1960s, the immigration laws in 1965 made it easier for foreigners to enter Western countries. In addition, Vatican II, an important ecumenical council held by Christian authorities in the same year, called for all Christians to be tolerant of other religions. This gave additional impetus for Hindus to come to the West. This time, however, it was not merely well meaning but unfortunate people looking for a better life, nor was it the philosophical texts—the abstract "emigrants"—who precipitated the third wave. Rather, the new Hindu "diaspora" (and this continues to the present day) consists of educated middle- and upper-class urbanites.[2] These are professionals— doctors, engineers, computer programmers, and so on—settling in posh, higher class neighborhoods and not in ethnic ghettoes. Hindus are here to stay, penetrating all strata of society.

WORLDWIDE DEMOGRAPHICS

Predictably, 98.6 percent of the world's Hindus (about 1 billion) still reside in South Asia. The largest number of Hindus is in India, with almost 800 million practitioners. In Nepal, however, which has a significantly smaller number of Hindus (about 19 million), they account for a greater percentage of the overall population. Nepal, in fact, is the only "Hindu" state in the world, or officially claimed as such. Sri Lanka and Bangladesh also boast a significant portion of Hindus, as do Burma, Malaysia, Singapore, Indonesia, and the Middle East.

A large number of Hindu practitioners also reside in South America and in the Caribbean, including the countries of Guyana, Surinam, Trinidad, and Tobago. Interestingly, Surinamese Indians constitute 37 percent of the population of their country, and at least 82 percent of them are Hindus. In Guyana, Indians make up more than half of the population, with Hinduism being embraced by 60 percent. Throughout the Caribbean, one finds immigrant Indians who practice various forms of the Hindu religion.

Indians from India make up about 3 percent of the total population of South Africa, which translates into about 1 million people. Approximately 65 percent of them are Hindus, 15 percent are Muslims, and the remainder are Christians. They have mainly settled in the eastern regions of Natal and Transvaal. The small island of Mauritius, off the coast of South Africa, is more than 50 percent Hindu. Great Britain and the United States also have significant but much smaller Hindu populations,

Table 4.1
Hindu Population by Continent

Africa	1,535,000
Europe	1,522,000
Asia	800,000,000
Latin America	748,000
North America	1,185,000
Oceania	305,000

Source: UN medium variant figures for mid-1995, as given in World Population Prospects: The 1994 Revision (1995), or see http://www.zpub.com/un/pope/relig.html.

with "English" Hindus numbering about 400,000 and "Hindu-Americans" just over 1 million.[3]

In Europe, Great Britain is the only country with a significant Hindu community, although the Hindu population in the Netherlands is growing as well. However, Europe is home to famous centers of Asian and African studies, with a special focus in Hinduism. In addition to the famous one in England, affiliated with the University of London, these can be found in Utrecht (the Netherlands), Helsinki (Finland), Berlin (Germany), and Vienna (Austria).

Surprisingly, the Oceania region, with a central focus on Australia and New Zealand, has traditionally followed a "whites only" policy, excluding most Asians from that part of the world. In recent years, however, it has relaxed its immigration laws, allowing more Asians, including Indians, to settle there. More than 400,000 Indians are now in Oceania, and most of them are Hindus, still adhering to the same forms of Hinduism as practiced in India. Fiji, in particular, is almost 50 percent Hindu.

Countries with the fewest Hindus include Thailand, which is 95 percent Buddhist, Malaysia, Singapore, Oman, Yemen, and, surprisingly, Pakistan, which is mainly Muslim (Table 4.1).

Worldwide, Hinduism breaks down to 70 percent Vaishnavas, 25 percent Shaivites (and Shaktas), 2 percent neo-Hindus, with the balance being reform Hindus of various small sects.[4]

HINDUISM OUTSIDE INDIA

For Indian Hindus, it is not always easy to practice the religion outside of India. Scriptural mandates specify certain regions in India as particularly sacred. Certain practices, social customs, and general patterns and modes of behavior are easier when living in the land of the Ganges. Still, Indians by and large have made due with facilities and locales thousands of miles from their homeland. An understanding of Hindu teachings and rituals (as outlined in Chapter 2) can afford some idea of how the indigenous traditions of India might adapt to new worlds and the modern milieu of Western countries. Hindu cosmology and philosophy are all-encompassing and universal and so should have no problem making itself practicable in alien environments. And this is important to Hindus: they want not only to adapt their tradition to the modern world, but to keep the practices and ways of their ancestors. In spite of the uncertainties produced by modernity and migration, age-old rituals reinforce a certain continuity with the past, bringing the old world into the new and allowing practitioners to take advantage of the time-tested traditions.

The Hindu system of religions includes facility for reconstructing sacred landscapes in the modern world, in lands and environments that are far from traditional Indian holy places. The construction of temples that are consistent with the cosmology found in traditional Hindu texts or those that seem in tangible ways to be connected with the sacred spaces of India allow even the most traditionalist practitioners to build modern places of worship in a new world.[5]

There are at least four different ways by which Hindus have made areas of the Western world ritually sacred and, to some extent, ritually continuous with the land of India: (1) adapting Sanskrit cosmology by identifying Western regions as associated with or corresponding to similar places in India; (2) composing songs and pious Sanskrit prayers extolling the Western soil where the new temples are located; (3) physically consecrating the land with waters from sacred Indian rivers; and (4) literally recreating the physical landscape of certain holy places in India, as Hindus have done in Pittsburgh, or Barsana Dham, near Austin, Texas.[6]

Overall, Hindus practice Hinduism in standard ways, regardless of where they might find themselves. For example, many Hindus are vegetarian, and because of this (among other factors) vegetarian restaurants have surged in popularity, even in the West. Ayurveda, or a form of holistic healing that originates in the Hindu scriptures, is now practiced around the world, with courses now available at both universities and hospitals. Yoga and meditation originated in ancient India as techniques for spiritual development and were developed by Hindu sages. These practices are now commonplace the world over, whether or not one is a believing Hindu.

SAMSKARAS, OR HINDU SACRAMENTS

Wherever Hindus find themselves, they do certain things that characterize their relationship with the world around them and certain activities that mark them as distinctly Hindu. One such collage of activities is known as *Samskaras,* a word that basically means "impressions." The idea is that certain activities leave impressions in the heart that stay with people for lifetimes, defining them as spiritual beings and as functional members of society. These are actions that, according to Hindu tradition, separate people from animals. They are rites of passage, clearly formulated rituals meant to help a person progress toward the ultimate goal of life.

Certain prayers and ceremonies are performed at particularly pivotal points in a given Hindu's life, which would make them equivalent to Christian sacraments. There are, in fact, 16 such sacraments, at least major ones, ranging from conception to funeral ceremonies:

1. Life begins with the sacrament of impregnation, that is, prayers for the conception of a healthy and spiritually evolved child.
2. Similar prayers and ceremonies are held in the second or third month of pregnancy, for the well-being of the child.
3. The same prayers and ceremonies are held again between the fifth and eighth month of pregnancy.
4. The same prayers and ceremonies are held again when the child is being born.
5. Naming the child is an important ceremony with special prayers.
6. Next, there is a ceremony commemorating the child's first steps out of the house, in the third or fourth month of the child's life.
7. The first feeding of cereal to the child at 6 months old is celebrated in various ways.
8. The first hair-cutting ceremony is performed during the first or third year of the child's life.
9. Piercing the ears in the third or fifth year accompanies certain prayers and festivities.
10. Investiture of a sacred thread, during the eighth year, signifies class status.
11. A special ceremony ensues when studies are completed.
12. The Hindu marriage ceremony is a special occasion with specific prayers according to social status.
13. There are special sacraments to be adhered to by married couples.
14. A special ceremony is conducted for renouncing married life and becoming serious about preparing for death and enhancing one's spiritual resolve.

15. Complete renunciation includes the vows and ceremony associated with the final spiritual stage of life.
16. The funeral, usually cremation, is the final sacrament, consisting of an elaborate system of last rites for the dead. Traditionally, the sacrament of death calls for the burning of the body (although dedicated renunciants and infants who die prematurely are buried), after which the ashes are dispersed in a holy river. The symbolic gesture means that the body goes back to the earth, to the material elements from whence it came; but the soul, which comes from God, is given back to Him. It is said that if any part of the body remains, the soul may, out of attachment, linger in the material world. Pious Hindus thus make certain that the cremation is thorough. Moreover, they ascertain that the ashes are indeed scattered in a holy river, or placed at some other holy site, for if these ashes remain in some material environment, the soul might stay along with them.

For 10 days after cremation (or sometimes 12 days, or 1 year, or once a year, depending on the sect), a senior male in the family must offer balls of rice to the deceased. The food grain symbolizes sustenance and concern and is meant to provide the departed with a body in which to dwell in the world of the ancestors. Otherwise, while waiting for his or her next birth, the late family member is said to wander in the world of ghosts—disembodied beings who are cursed to subtle existence, without body or senses, between the world we know and darker regions. These postdeath rituals are required only of the Hindu householder and do not apply to the renunciant.

Not all Hindus observe the Samskaras, but most do, at least in one form or another. Whether or not all of these 16 sacraments are observed, they are always part of the underlying premise of Hindu practices in general, and they remain in the background of the average Hindu's life, informing his or her day-to-day work and relationship with the world.

PRACTICE IN GENERAL

Daily worship in Hinduism usually takes place in three different arenas: in the home, in a temple, and/ or at a street-side or roadside shrine. The street shrines are mainly found in India. Most religious life is at home, even if temple and road-side shrines offer similar facility for practice, and usually on a grander scale. At home, Hindus usually reserve a room or special section of their dwelling for worship. Such worship is called *puja* and is centered on an image or picture of God (in any of His or Her many manifestations) and a picture of their guru, or teacher, as well. (See Deity Worship).

Those who are particularly strict rise before dawn, take a bath (for purposes of cleanliness but also for ritual purification), and begin their daily ceremonial functions. Higher-caste Hindus then chant special prayers, or incantations, with the rising of the sun. They repeat these prayers at midday and as the sun goes down, commemorating God's pervasive nature and His (or Her) paramount place in their lives throughout each day. The head of the household (or gifted orators at the temple) reads from sacred texts and comments on the insights of the sages.

Food and drink, usually with flowers and incense, are offered at the home shrine, too, and the remnants of the offering are taken as the family meal. Larger quantities of food are offered at temple locations and then distributed to all who attend. Such consecrated food, known as *prasadam*, is central in Hindu thought. The idea is that everything one has should be offered back to God in gratitude, as it all comes from Him (or Her) in the first place. Also, this home and temple worship accomplishes another end in Hindu philosophy. Because it is taught that all the senses are to be engaged in God's service, the picture or image of God on the altar engages the eyes, the incense and flowers engage the sense of smell, the offered food engages the sense of taste, and so on.

SOME KEY HINDU PRACTICES

Deity Worship

One of the most misunderstood aspects of modern Hinduism is deity worship, that is, the peculiar form of temple or home worship where a human being offers food, flowers, water, and love to a "statue" made of material elements—the process of *puja*. What would inspire a rational human being to bow down to a mere statue as if it were God? This question is asked by the average Hindu as well. Hinduism is as much against idol worship as is the modern Westerner; however, idol worship is in the eye of the outside observer.

In Hinduism, deities are fashioned according to strict outlines in the scriptures, depicting Krishna, Rama, Vishnu, or others, as revealed by the sages who have seen these divinities directly. Thus, it is not that Hindu images are constructed according to someone's fanciful imagination. Indeed, *this* would be idol worship. Instead, Hindus rely on authorized sources and a special ceremony, in which the Lord Himself agrees to come down and accept worship through objects that ordinary mortals can see. In fact, the deity has been referred to as among the most merciful of divine manifestations specifically *because* he manifests in a form of material elements, a form that people can serve, love, admire, and interact with. Thus, he becomes particularly accessible in his deity form, and, through this form, most Hindus are able to develop a closeness with God.

Brief mention should be made of the English word *idol*. An idol, by definition, is an imaginary representation, a counterfeit god, concocted by a mortal mind. Hinduism teaches that deities, or the apparently material forms that appear in homes and temples, are *not* idols because they are based on the revelations of scriptures and self-realized sages. These forms are not the products of colorful fiction or overactive imaginations. Still, when the British came to India, they used the word *idol* to refer to Hindu deities. This reference is now known to have been conscious; it was a part of the British strategy to disparage Hindu religion. In this way, they sought to weaken Hindu self-perceptions and thereby succeed with their political agenda of invasion and occupation. Many Hindus unconsciously adopted the term from the British and have been using it ever since, not realizing that it refers to a "false god" and that it has a multitude of pejorative implications.

Yoga

All Hindus practice yoga, but not all Hindus practice Raja yoga, or the path of physical exercise, sitting postures, and meditation that most Westerners associate with it. In other words, there are various kinds of yoga. Because the Raja yoga system is described in eight steps (Table 4.2), it is sometimes called Ashtanga yoga, "the eightfold path," but it is more commonly known as Hatha yoga. The word *yoga* comes from the Sanskrit root *yuj*, which means "to link up with, to combine." It is similar to *religio*, the Latin root of the word *religion*, which means "to bind together." Religion and yoga, then, have the same end in mind: linking with God.

Yoga was systematized in medieval India by a sage named Patanjali in his Yoga sutras, a text that explains the methodical process whereby one can learn to control the body and mind, with the ultimate goal of using these finely tuned material instruments in the service of the Lord. In yoga the body is viewed as the temple of the soul. By means of postures (*asanas*) and breath control (*pranayama*), yoga promotes physical health and mental well-being that help strengthen the "temple." In the West, the physical fitness part of it has become an end in itself. According to the traditional

Table 4.2
The Yoga System: The 8 Steps of Ashtanga-Yoga

Remote Preparation
1. *yama* (practice of precepts)
   • nonviolence
   • truthfulness
   • not stealing
   • continence
   • absence of greed
2. *niyama* (practice of virtues)
   • purity
   • peacefulness
   • discipline
   • study, especially of sacred texts
   • surrender to God
3. postures
4. breath control
5. withdrawal of the senses

Direct Preparation
6. concentration
7. meditation
8. spiritual trance

Advanced Practice
The exercise of extraordinary powers and the practice of advanced forms of meditation, leading to "perfection" (complete absorption and freedom).

yoga system, however, this was merely the first step on the path of God realization.

In the Bhagavad Gita, Arjuna, the ultimate yogi, tells Krishna, the Lord, that Raja yoga is too difficult in this age, that it takes more than a single lifetime to perfect the process, and that people in this age are too distracted to properly execute the rigors of yoga proper. Krishna concurs and outlines numerous alternate yogic paths, the most important being the Yoga of Work, the Yoga of Knowledge, and the Yoga of Love. In the sixth chapter of the Bhagavad Gita, Krishna tells Arjuna not to worry about the difficulties associated with yoga, for he, Arjuna, is already the best of yogis. This is so because, as Krishna tells him, of all yogis, the best is he who performs the Yoga of Love: "Of all yogis, the one with great faith, who always abides in Me, thinks of Me within himself, and renders transcendental loving service to Me—he is the most intimately united with Me in yoga and is the highest of all." Most Hindus are Vaishnavas, so they generally perform some aspect of the Yoga of Love.

Meditation

Meditation is a natural corollary of yoga, and all Hindus practice this in one form or another. Traditional yogic systems use complex meditation techniques as frequently as sitting postures, because both are useful in developing a sound body and mind. To quiet the mind and to provide a point of focus, the spiritual aspirant concentrates on various holy images and sacred forms. Most commonly, however, they focus on *mantras,* sacred sounds, ranging from mere Sanskrit syllables to names of God. Vaishnava texts recommend the names of God as particularly effective in the current age, superseding all other forms of meditation.

In most Hindu systems, therefore, emphasis is placed on three distinct forms of practice: *japa, kirtan,* and *sankirtan.* In *japa* the practitioner softly recites to himself or herself God's name with the use of a rosary (*japa-mala*), usually consisting of 108 beads. *Kirtan,* on the other hand, is a "public meditation," in which one loudly sings the name of God, often accompanied by musical instruments and dancing. When performed in a group, with other worshipers, this is called *Sankirtan.* This is considered the most efficacious process of God realization in the current age. As the sacred texts say, "What was obtained in the Satya Age, the earliest age, by meditation on Vishnu, in the Treta Age, the next age, by elaborate sacrifice, in the Dvapara Age, the prior age, by image worship, comes in the Kali Age, our current age, through chanting the name of Krishna."[7]

As meditation evolves, the practitioner develops his or her inner life. In the meditational technique known as *pastime remembrance,* the aspirant chiefly focuses on the names, form, qualities, and pastimes of the Lord—as delineated in the scriptures and understood from the words of the teacher, who has "seen" the truth—often along with renewed enthusiasm for chanting the holy name of the Lord. The practitioner begins such meditation by chanting God's name in a regulated way, under the guidance of a spiritual master. The beginner generally has little ability to concentrate, yet due to study of scripture and sincerity of purpose, even at this early stage one can acquire a preliminary memory of God in the spiritual world. With the inner longing to gain focus, the ability to concentrate develops. The enhanced familiarity with God's pastimes leads to the next level, in which the practitioner learns to meditate in a more direct way, by placing oneself in the midst of God's holy activity, gradually developing expertise in visualizing the pastimes of the Lord. Becoming accomplished in this art, the practitioner learns to meditate without interference, and throughout the day can focus on the object of meditation without substantial distraction. The final stage entails complete absorption, wherein one comes face to face with the Deity and is situated in a separate reality.

Noninjury (Ahimsa)

Ahimsa refers to nonviolence, or, more specifically, to nonaggression, and it is a high priority in the practice of Hinduism (see also Chapter 2). Indeed, the scriptures (Mahabharata 13.116.37–4) say that *"Ahimsa* is the highest duty," meaning that qualities such as gentleness, humility, and compassion—and all related qualities—are necessary components of spiritual life, without which, one is not really practicing Hinduism proper. Buddhism and Jainism, two primary heterodoxies of traditional Hinduism, have elevated *ahimsa* even further, considering it a central teaching.

Ahimsa is supposed to be practiced not only on the physical level, but also on mental and emotional levels. It asks that practitioners avoid abusiveness, whether overtly or in more subtle ways.

Generally, *ahimsa* is associated with animal protection and vegetarianism, which is observed by a vast majority of believing Hindus. Even those who are not vegetarian usually view it as a high ideal. Devout Hindus oppose killing for many reasons. They know that every action holds within it an avoidable reaction (karma), and the idea of reincarnation is never far from the Hindu mind. Thus, believe Hindus, what they have done to others will be done to them—that is the universal law of cause and effect. In other words, killing begets killing, and because there are many lives in which to reap that which one sows, violence and killing are eventually thrust upon anyone who is violent or who kills, if not in this life then in the next one.

Two thousand years ago, South India's weaver saint, Tiruvalluvar, claimed, "All suffering recoils on the wrongdoer himself. Thus, those desiring not to suffer refrain from causing pain to others."[8] The idea is echoed in the Jain work, the Acharanga Sutra: "To do harm to others is to do harm to oneself. You are in essence he whom you intend to kill. You are also he whom you intend to dominate. We corrupt ourselves as soon as we intend to corrupt others. We kill ourselves as soon as we intend to kill others." These ideas blend the teachings of *ahimsa* and karma into one tightly knit tapestry, one that is hung in the home of all believing Hindus.

But Hindus embrace *ahimsa* for more than merely self-motivated reasons. They seek to develop qualities like compassion and kindness because these things are virtuous in their own right. It is not that they are simply interested in avoiding a backlash for violent or thoughtless activity. To understand the pervasive practice of nonviolence in Hinduism, one must understand how Hindus view the life-force itself. Why is life sacred? For India's ancient thinkers, life is part of God, an emanation of the Divine that must be respected and honored. Love for God cannot be attained if one does not develop love for God's children, for the sparks of divinity that flow from His (or Her) essence. Accordingly, Hindus have a natural reverence for life, which is part and parcel of their reverence for God.

But Hinduism is practical when it comes to nonviolence. It teaches that while nonviolence is a virtue, it needs to be practiced with common sense, and its limitations should be known. In India, there is a saying: "It is a sin to kill the tiger in the jungle. But if he comes into the village, it may become your duty to kill him." It was for reasons such as this that Hindu society was traditionally divided into different castes: A priest or intellectual was never expected to kill, under any circumstance, but an administrator or warrior might kill to protect, and in this way society could move forward peacefully. Naturally, even the administrator/warrior was expected to have a sense of *ahimsa*, and, if he could, he was expected to resolve problems through peaceful means. In the case of a wild tiger invading a village, for example, he was obliged to first try to sway the tiger from its human prey by leading her away from the people. But if this could not be done, he was expected to protect the citizens by any means necessary. In such a situation, with great caution, violence could be used for a greater good.

Cow Protection

Most Hindus are natural supporters of cow protection, which is intimately related to the concept of *ahimsa*, or nonviolence. Despite popular belief, there is no formal worship of a "cow-goddess" in Hindu temples. Rather, the cow is respected in her own right as one of humankind's seven mothers because she offers her milk as does one's natural mother.[9] Mahatma Gandhi, one of India's great political thinkers, had the highest regard for cows: "To me, the cow is the embodiment of the whole infra-human world; she enables the believer to grasp his unity with all that lives.... To protect her is to protect all the creatures of God's creation."[10]

As cows play a central role in India's economy, the five products of the cow—milk, curd, *ghee* (clarified butter), urine, and dung—are all considered purifying and useful. The dairy products are consumed, and even cow dung is useful, serving as an inexpensive fertilizer. It is sometimes stored in underground tanks, where it generates methane gas that is used for heating and cooking. Cow dung is also a valuable disinfectant and is used both as a poultice and a cleansing agent. Cow urine, in its own way, is equally valuable. It is a natural and fully biodegradable cleanser and proven disinfectant (with an extremely high ammonia content). Cow urine is also useful as an ingredient in any number of Ayurvedic medicines.

Where did this high regard for the cow originate? Traditionally, she was considered dear to Lord Krishna. Indeed, Krishna is often known as "Gopal" and "Govinda"—names that refer to his loving feeling for cows. The very names of Krishna's holy land of Braj ("pasture") and his spiritual abode Goloka ("cow-world") reveal his intimate connection with bovine creatures. His love for the cow is celebrated throughout the Vedic literature. It is no wonder, therefore, that in the Vedas there is great emphasis on *ahimsa*, or harmlessness to all sentient beings, and especially on cow protection.

The Vedic reference book Nighantu offers nine Sanskrit names for the cow, three of which—*aghnya* ("not to be killed"), *ahi* ("not be killed"), and *aditi* ("not to be cut")—specifically forbid slaughter. These synonyms for "cow" are summarized in the epic work Mahabharata: "The very name of the cows is *aghnya*, indicating that they should never be slaughtered. Who, then, could slay them? Surely, one who kills a cow or a bull commits the most heinous crime."[11]

Dress

Part of Hindu practice involves clothing. In India, like everywhere, clothing functions as an important marker of social classification. People communicate their identity and beliefs through the wearing of particular clothes, with various regional nuances in style. In general, the traditional dress for both men and women consists of various cloths elegantly draped over the body and held together by folds and tucks. In place of trousers (which, with modernity, are becoming more common) men wear the age-old *dhoti*—a loosely draped waistcloth, and a *kurta*—a long, loose-fitting shirt. The way in which the *dhoti* is folded on the body reveals whether a man is a renunciant, a celibate student, or a husband. Many Hindus in the West do not wear the traditional dress in public, although many change into special devotional clothes when they attend worship services.

The *sari*, a single-length of draped cloth, usually quite colorful and exotic looking, is still the most popular form of dress for women, both in India and abroad. Different draping methods reveal the part of the country from which a woman comes and often the tradition with which she is associated. The color of one's dress, especially with men, is a clear indicator of social status. Senior renunciants and students tend to wear saffron (representing celibacy), whereas householders (married men) generally wear white. White is also the color of dress for women who are widowed, in contrast to the bright colors and patterns of married women's saris.

Most Hindus also wear various kinds of neck beads, not merely for ornamental purposes but as an indication of religious commitment. A three-strand necklace of *tulasi* beads, for example, indicates that one has accepted a spiritual teacher (guru). In addition to these sartorial components, hairstyle and bodily markings are also used as indicators of religious affiliation. Vaishnava monks generally have shaven heads, keeping only a tuft of hair on the back of the head. This distinguishes them from Buddhists and the followers of Shankara, whose heads are completely shaven.

A woman is viewed as either a prostitute or a respectable person depending on the manner in which she parts her hair. Forehead markings are another essential element of identification in Vaishnava and Shaivite culture. Married women wear a red dot in the center of the forehead (*bindi*). Today many young girls and unmarried women wear similar *bindis* in many colors, but these have no religious or social meaning.

The markings called *tilak*, or *tika*, are applied to various parts of the body with sacred clay or sandalwood paste in styles that distinguish followers of one spiritual lineage from another. These markings are said to consecrate the body as a temple of God, so the believing Hindu applies them each morning, or at least before going to their place of worship. Devotees of Shiva use this clay to paint three horizontal lines on their foreheads, whereas Vaishnavas paint two vertical lines, often with a leaflike shape at the bottom, by the tip of their nose. Most Hindus in the West do not wear these markings on the outside but apply it to their bodies only before worship services.

Pilgrimage

Visiting holy places is an important component in the practice of Hinduism. Every pious Hindu hopes to at least once in his or her life visit Benares, the holy city of Lord Shiva, or perhaps Gomukh, the sacred source of the Ganges, high in the Himalayas. Many areas of the Himalayas, in fact, are eulogized in India's sacred texts for their sacredness and solitude—just the perfect sort of places for meditation and reflection on the Lord.

For most Hindus, important sites include the "the seven cities," also known as "the cities that award liberation." These are Ayodhya, Mathura, Haridwar, Benares (mentioned previously), Kanchi, Ujjain, and Dvaraka. Indian texts also focus on seven sacred rivers: the Ganges, Yamuna, Godavari, Sarasvati, Narmada, Sindhu, and Kaveri. To go to any of these areas is to achieve an immediate benediction. In fact, Hindu theology opines that only special souls are allowed entrance to these regions, and one who manages to arrive there, it is believed, has truly "arrived" in a spiritual sense. Hindu texts opine that these locales are imbued with special spiritual potency, and that the purification derived from even the most brief visit is incalculable.

The most important pilgrimage sites for Vaishnavas, devotees of Vishnu, are Braj (Vrindavan, which is in the Mathura region), Mayapur, and Jagannath Puri. These are considered replicas of various parts of the spiritual world, manifesting in the realm of three dimensions simply to whet the sojourner's appetite, to beckon practitioners to go back home, back to Godhead. Also significant are Shri Rangam, Tirupati, Guruvayur, and many others in the South. Although such holy places can ultimately be reached only by internal meditation and intense devotion, or so say the scriptures, one may begin one's journey by exploring these external manifestations of the spiritual realm, conveniently located in modern-day India for pilgrims to visit.

NOTES

1. See Cybelle Shattuck (adapted by Nancy D. Lewis), *The Pocket Idiot's Guide to Hinduism* (Indianapolis: Alpha Books, 2003), pp. 142–143.

2. Ibid.

3. Some of these statistics can be found in Russell Ash, *The Top 10 of Everything* (New York: DK Publishing, 1997), pp. 160–161. Also see www. adherents.com. For more, see Barry A. Kosmin and Seymour P. Lachman, *One Nation Under God: Religion in Contemporary American Society* (New York: Harmony Books, 1993). Also see http://www.adherents.com/largercom/com_hindu.html.

4. Ibid. Regarding the overwhelmingly large number of Vaishnavas, it does not necessarily refer to those who worship Vishnu exclusively but can also include those who see him as one god among many, even if they tend to favor him for one reason or another.

5. For more on this phenomenon, see Vasudha Narayanan, "Heterogeneous Spaces and Modernities: Hindu Rituals to Sacralize the American Landscape" in *Journal of Vaishnava Studies*, 13 (2005): 127–148.

6. Ibid.

7. Shrimad Bhagavatam 12.3.52.

8. Tirukural 320.

9. The other six mothers of Hinduism are (1) one's biological mother; (2) the nurse who cares for the infant; (3) the spiritual master's wife; (4) the wife of a Brahmin; (5) the Vedas, or the ancient scriptures of India; and (6) the Earth (or, alternatively, the wife of the king).

10. Sushil Patel, *The Words of the Mahatma: A Collection* (Delhi: One Place Books, 2000), p. 5.1.

11. Shanti-parva 262.47.

5

RITUALS AND HOLIDAYS

In modern Hinduism, there are many holidays and festival days, with several celebrated on any given day. All Hindu holidays are festive, and so, in the Indic tradition, the words "festival" and "holiday" are more or less synonymous, although each emphasizes a different aspect of the days' events. All holidays are festivals, and all festivals take place on days that are considered holidays, or days that are particularly auspicious for glorifying the Lord.

This latter point has special meaning in Hinduism because the vast majority of India's many holidays have a strong religious component, and to this day they remain undiluted by the kind of consumerism and self-centered party-going found in the West. As such, Hinduism remains a potent spiritual force, virtually untouched by the secular, postmodern world. There may be pros and cons to this determined attachment to tradition, but the net result is that Hinduism's festivals and holidays are practiced in much the same way as they were hundred of years ago, if not thousands.

Some Hindu holidays are more modern and several have no religious significance. For example, there are four well-known National holidays in India. These are observed by all Hindus, regardless of sectarian affiliation, and government institutions acknowledge them in all Indian states:

- Republic Day, January 26
- Labor Day, May 1
- Independence Day, August 15
- Gandhi Jayanti, October 2

This fourth holiday is the birth anniversary of Mahatma Gandhi, the political "Father of the Nation." Special prayers and celebrations are offered at the Gandhi Tomb at Rajghat, Delhi, and parties are held throughout the country.[1] But the vast majority of Hinduism's holidays are religious. As in the West, most holidays are observed annually, but some occur only at rare intervals. And some, in fact, happen only in special places. The huge Kumbha Mela, for example, when millions of Hindus gather at the confluence of the Ganges and Yamuna Rivers, takes place once every 12 years, although there are smaller melas that occur more frequently. That is, the festival actually occurs four times every 12 years at special locations in the subcontinent. At the culmination of each 12-year cycle there is a "Great" Kumbha Mela at Prayag, attended by millions of people, making it the largest festival gathering around the world. Again, these are not merely festivals, for all Hindu festivals are also holidays. But these, at least, are holidays that are best celebrated in certain areas, and so numerous families take the day (or week) off work and school to attend at the prescribed locations. Sometimes these holidays are re-created in other parts of the country or in other parts of the world, but they are most effectively observed at the traditional locale.

Of the annual holidays, the 2-day celebration of Holi marks the end of winter and announces the beginning of spring. Unlike the Kumbha Mela, this holiday can be honored anywhere, but it is unlikely that one will find it enacted as vigorously as in North India. Holi is associated with Lord Krishna, God in humanlike form, whose loving activities with the cowherd maidens of Braj, his greatest devotees, are commemorated at that time. With a light heart and a spirit of unabashed frivolity, devotees at this time shoot colored dyes at each other, just as Krishna had done with his cowherd girlfriends. The holiday also commemorates the killing of a demoness named Holika, who is said to have terrorized the earth, according to certain of India's ancient historical accounts. So this holiday honors two quite diverse aspects of Hindu lore. It is a time of joy, celebration, and hope for the future. The Kumbha Mela and Holi are two of the most anticipated holidays on the Hindu calendar.

In general, Hindu holidays include a wide variety of rituals, including worship, prayer, processions, dramatic performance, magical acts, music, dancing, feasting, and feeding the poor. Such joyous Hindu festivals perhaps best sum up what Hinduism is really all about. Often denigrated by its critics as an "otherworldly" religion, obsessed with the afterlife, Hindu festivals and holidays show how grounded in this world Hindus actually are. True, their interests lie in spiritual pursuits and otherworldly concerns, but these are preoccupations that clearly manifest in the here-and-now, with a sophisticated merriment sensibility and grassroots attention to sensual delights. Indeed, in celebrating the Lord, Hindus show a marked sense of aesthetics that includes lavishly decorated temples and festival sites; the exotic fragrance of flowers and incense; the beautiful vision of the iconic form of the Lord, tastefully decorated with ornate jewelry and elegant clothing; and the sounds of timeless songs and holy invocations. It is a virtual demonstration in how to engage the world of three dimensions in spiritual activity without reservation. Hindus, too, are anything but bashful and often bring their enchanting holidays onto the streets, engaging onlookers and curious bystanders in performing celebratory rituals, like it or not. It brings a smile to many a face.

These celebrations are interpreted according to one's devotion, according to exactly which of the Hindu religions one observes. In other words, worshippers of Shiva (Shaivites), Vishnu (Vaishnavas), or the Goddess (Shaktas), for example, may take the same festival and give it a unique spin, according to the theology of their particular group. Or they may honor various aspects of a holiday, or different holidays on the same day. In late September or early October, for instance, Shaivites and Shaktas will celebrate Durga Puja, a special ceremony in honor of the Goddess (which will be explored more fully later in this chapter), while Vaishnavas, on the same day, will take part in a festival known as Dussehra, which celebrates Vishnu and his exploits as Rama in the Ramayana. Similarly, Divali, "the festival of lights," is celebrated either as the return of Rama from exile or as the veneration of Lakshmi, the goddess of wealth and fortune, depending on the lineage or sect with which one affiliates.

India is often called a land where there are "13 religious festivals in 12 months." Again, the vastness of the Hindu tradition allows for almost daily festivities. The scale of such celebrations may range from a *mahotsava* ("large festival") to a simple gathering in the home. Every festival offers many layers of meaning, and they are edifying in numerous ways for the people who take part. Enthusiastic practitioners perform and attend festivals to purify themselves, to obtain the blessings of sages, to receive religious instruction, and to experience a joyful respite from everyday life.[2]

THE HINDU CALENDAR

Festival dates are observed in accordance with the Hindu calendar, which is calculated by the phases of the moon rather than by the orbit of the sun, the latter of which is the way it is done in the West. As such, if one uses the traditional Gregorian calendar, as is done in the West, the dates of Hindu holidays appear to change each year. Add to this that Hindu calendars vary according to regional considerations, and the net result is that one must be something of an expert to really comprehend the Hindu calendar system. A basic understanding of this system—or at least a basic understanding that such a system exists—is crucial to perceiving just when and how Hindus observe their religious holidays.

All Hindu calendars originate from the Jyotish Vedanga (one of the six Vedic adjuncts, said to have been composed just before the Common Era). Some form of standardization occurred centuries later when sages consulted the Surya Siddhanta, a text dealing with astronomy and astrological sciences, and it was further adjusted by astronomers in as late as the sixteenth century. In 1957, The Indian Calendar Reform Committee finalized the Indian National Calendar, along with a specifically religious calendar—the Rashtriya Panchang. This endeavor was mainly undertaken to determine the holidays of government workers and to standardize when shops should close and school children should have days off.

Moreover, this official Indian calendar is based on solar reckoning, even if its calculation originates with the Surya Siddhanta, which is generally given to lunar considerations. Months are calculated according to the sun's position against fixed stars or constellations during sunrise. The sun's position here is understood by diametrically opposed observations of the full moon. This sort of computation sidesteps the necessity of leap year adjustments, but the number of days in any given month can vary by nearly 48 hours, and conversion of dates to Gregorian or day of the week computations requires the use of an ephemeris. The lay person therefore relies on the *panchangs* or almanacs produced by authoritative astronomical schools.[3]

The word *panchang* is derived from the Sanskrit *panchangam* (*pancha* = five, *anga* = limb), which refers to the five limbs of the calendar: (1) the lunar day, (2) the solar day, (3) the asterism on which the sun rises, (4) the angle of the sun and moon, and (5) the half lunar day. Over time, various priestly groups who made it their business to produce the *panchang*s have favored different geographical centers, thus affecting numerous aspects of its astronomical calculation. This naturally resulted in a divergence of a few days, which is reflected in regional calendars. Even within the same region, there may be more than one competing authority, occasionally resulting in disagreement on festival dates by as much as a month.[4]

In most Indian calendars, another consideration is that of lunar *tithis,* which is basically the final part of the lunar month, although it runs concurrently with solar estimates. Birth dates and the like are recorded in solar terms, but the *tithis* determines the timing of the religious rituals associated with those events. Thus, every day is marked with a solar month and date, as well as a lunar *tithi,* corresponding to the position of the moon at sunrise. Given this excessiveness of detail, most people merely consult their local priests for the dates and times of religious holidays, thus avoiding the differences created by regional factors and other considerations. Still, if two Hindus, from various parts of the subcontinent, were to talk on the phone, they might find that the same holiday occurs for them at different times, that one is observing it while the other has to wait a day or two to observe the same festival.

EAST AND WEST: A CALENDAR BREAKDOWN

The 12 months of the lunar year correspond to the following calendar months and make up the six seasons of Hinduism:

1. Chaitra (March–April)
2. Vaishakha (April–May)   Vasanta (Spring)
3. Jyeshtha (May–June)
4. Ashadh (June–July)   Greeshma (Summer)
5. Shravana (July–August)
6. Bhadrapad (August–September)   Varsha (Monsoon)
7. Ashvin (September–October)
8. Kartik (October–November)   Sharad (Autumn)
9. Margasheersh (November–December)
10. Paush (December–January)   Hemanta (Winter)
11. Magh (January–February)
12. Phalguna (February–March)   Shishira (Dewey)

SPECIAL HOLIDAYS

The more important Hindu festivals and holidays, along with a brief description of their meaning, are explained here. This is by no means a thorough list, as Hindu holidays are as vast as the waves of an ocean.

In the month of Magh (January–February) the Magh Mela, a sort of Vaishnava counterpart to the much larger Kumbha Mela, takes place. People come from all over India to special predetermined areas (although many celebrate this festival in their homes). Here, they bathe in holy rivers, immerse themselves in the glories of the Lord with song and dance, and perform many austerities to get closer to God. Such austerities might include chanting a large number of God's holy names—taking a full day (or several days) to perform—or a vow of silence or intense yogic disciplines.

Also in Magh, just before the onset of Phalguna (February–March), all of India also witnesses the massive Maha Shivaratri, one of the subcontinent's largest festivals. This is a time when Shaivites and Shaktas, devotees of Shiva and the Goddess, respectively, glorify the Lord with great intensity, vigorously chanting his name and performing penance on his behalf. Although Maha Shivaratri is not a Vaishnava holiday as such, many Vaishnavas honor Shiva as an alternate aspect of Vishnu, or, at the very least, as one of Vishnu's greatest devotees, and so they come together at this time to praise him as well.

In Phalguna (February–March), two special festivals mark the Indian calendar: Gaura Purnima (the appearance anniversary of Sri Chaitanya Mahaprabhu, Krishna in the guise of his own devotee) and Holi (a festival that celebrates the advent of spring, as mentioned previously). On Holi, people energetically spray each other with colored dyes, as stated, commemorating one of Krishna's many activities with the female cowherd devotees of Braj. Mahaprabhu's appearance day celebration, honoring his appearance in this world 500 years ago, is observed with fasting, feasting, prayer, chanting, and scriptural readings concerning his earthly pastimes.

Chaitra (March–April) is the time of Ramachandra's appearance in this world. He is an important incarnation of Vishnu, and celebrations with dramatic readings and performances of Sita and Rama's famous activities abound. Elaborate descriptions of Rama's love for Sita, her heartless kidnapping by the evil Ravana, the courage of Hanuman (Rama's half-monkey/half-man devotee) in bringing her Rama's message, Rama's battle with the king of demons—all are remembered in exacting detail. Throughout India, especially, all regions are engulfed in a barrage of plays, readings, chanting sessions and huge feasts in remembrance of the divine love of Sita and Rama.

As April turns to May, many Vaishnavas prepare for the appearance of Nrisimhadeva, the ferocious man-lion incarnation of the Lord. So in Vaishakha (April–May), the famous Nrisimha Chaturdashi is welcomed with stories and plays about the boy saint Prahlad and his relationship to Nrisimha. Beautiful costumes are made in which a dramatic actor plays the part of the half-man/half-lion incarnation, a young boy or girl will play

Prahlad (Nrisimhadeva's youthful devotee), and a masculine actor assumes the role of Hiranyakashipu, the demon who seeks to come between the Lord and his devotee. The performance evokes powerful emotions, showing the cruelty of Hiranyakashipu, the devotion of Prahlad, and both the fierce and compassionate sides of the Lord. All Hindus love this story and it is performed with various distinguishing nuances throughout the subcontinent. After the play, devotees rejoice with song and dance and a huge feast.

Jyeshtha (May–June) brings Buddha Purnima, which celebrates simultaneously Buddha's birth and enlightenment. Vaishnavas see Buddha as an incarnation of Vishnu, so they too take part in this festival, although they commemorate it in their own idiosyncratic way, usually by reading or performing Jayadeva's Gita Govinda, a beautiful twelfth-century poem that includes a special verse about Buddha as an incarnation of Vishnu. At this time, devotees also perform works of charity, give sermons on nonviolence, and otherwise lecture on Buddha's path to enlightenment.

Ashadh (June–July) is the time of the great Ratha-yatra festival at Puri, a celebratory procession that, through the efforts of the International Society for Krishna Consciousness (ISKCON), now takes place in cities all over the world. In Puri, millions come from throughout India to join in the festivities. Here, a distinct iconic form of Krishna in the form of Jagannath ("Lord of the Universe") rides atop a massive chariot, along with his sister,

Lord Jagannath's Ratha-yatra festival in Puri, India, where millions congregate to see the iconic form of Lord Krishna. Courtesy of the author.

Subhadra, and his brother, Balarama. This "sister" and "brother" are actually manifestations of his internal potency and his immediate expansion, respectively. This is perhaps the biggest festival of the Hindu world, second only to the Maha-Kumbha-Mela.

As the hot summer continues, Shravana (July–August) brings forth Naga Panchami, a glorification of Balarama (Krishna's elder brother) in his form of Shesha, the huge serpent who supports Vishnu with his divine coils. This is celebrated like most Hindu festivals, with readings, dramatic performance, singing, and feasting (often precipitated by fasting).

Bhadrapad (August–September) celebrates Krishna Janmashtami (the holy appearance of Shri Krishna). This month is also famous for Radhashtami, the divine birthday of Radha, Shri Krishna's consort. For Vaishnavas, God manifests on earth and, in so doing, He has "birthdays" and other celebrations for the satisfaction of his devotees, much as Jesus does in the Christian tradition. These days are special opportunities for devotees to remember the intimate pastimes of divine birth, which the Lord displays out of compassion for the souls of this world.

Another important festival during this month is Ganesh Chaturthi, the day of the elephant-headed god Ganesh. On this day, prayers are offered to the divine son of Lord Shiva. He is said to removes obstacles from one's spiritual life and is also considered the lord of thresholds. For this reason, his image is usually placed over doorways in observant Hindu homes and temples.

In Ashvin (September–October) there is a special festival connected to Durga Puja, as previously mentioned, and a long stream of diverse celebrations ending with the defeat of Ravana, the villain of the Ramayana. Ashvin is a time when Hindus remember that goodness wins out in the end; as such, throughout the streets of India gigantic effigies of the tyrant Ravana are set ablaze, proclaiming victory for all who are righteous.

Kartik (October–November) is celebrated as a month-long Vaishnava festival, during which Divali, the Festival of Lights, sometimes celebrated as the Hindu New Year, takes place, as do many others. This particular holiday venerates the day when Rama and Sita returned from their many years of hardship caused by the demonic Ravana. When they returned to their wonderful city of Ayodhya, the joy among the citizens was palpable, as if everyone had personally shared in their pain, which, in fact, they did. Lights were lit to celebrate the return of their king and queen, creating a beautiful atmosphere of divine victory over evil. Today, that feeling of victory is recreated by Hindus worldwide.

It is roughly at this time, too, that Govardhan Puja is celebrated, a festival that shows Krishna's supremacy over other gods. As the story goes,

Indra, the god of the heavens, was becoming overwhelmed with his own powers, forgetting his subservience to Krishna, or God. To challenge Krishna's supremacy, and to show his own, he sent torrential rains to devastate Krishna's ancestral village of Braj. Without batting an eye, Krishna lifted the enormous Mount Govardhan, using it as an umbrella to protect all of Braj's inhabitants—people, animals, trees, and so on. In this way, Krishna indicated that he is a force to be reckoned with, and this day commemorates this glorious event.

EKADASHI: THE DAY OF THE LORD

Throughout the Hindu year, there are festivals and holidays that begin with fasting and end with feasting. But Ekadashi, which occurs more than two dozen times throughout the Hindu year, is specifically for fasting. In Hinduism, both fasting and feasting are considered austerities that one performs for the Lord. Fasting is an austerity because one denies oneself food, and feasting is an austerity because it is considered mandatory to honor the foodstuffs offered to the deity, whether or not one enjoys them. It is a religious obligation, but a desirable one; the food is usually delectable.

Ekadashi is a celebratory holiday that falls regularly on the eleventh day after the new moon and after the full moon as well. The practice of Ekadashi starts at sunrise and lasts until the next sunrise. The main prohibition is against grains and beans, wherein sinful activity is said to reside on those particular days. In other words, if one eats grain or beans on the Ekadashi day, sin will permeate one's life. Therefore, Hindus refrain from these foods on the Ekadashi day. Some practice a more severe form of Ekadashi, fasting from all food, including water.

The idea of fasting is that a person should develop a sense of renunciation, of self-discipline, as well as gratefulness for the bounty of the Lord. This is how the austerity of fasting is specifically a *religious* obligation. It is also health-giving, allowing the body a time of rest, giving the usually overworked physical system a respite from mastication and digestion. Most of all, practitioners are expected to use the time that would have been devoted to cooking and eating to glorifying the Lord all the more.[5]

ELABORATION ON THREE HINDU HOLIDAYS

In Vaishnavism, or the worship of Vishnu (or Krishna, in any of his incarnations), the preeminent holiday is Janmashtami, or Krishna's appearance in the material world, his "birthday," which is said to have occurred roughly

5,000 years ago. Devotees are adamant about calling this an "appearance day" instead of a "birthday," because God, they say, is not compelled to take birth, as are ordinary souls. Rather, he "appears" in this world by his own sweet will, to share his charming activities with people who are fated to the material sphere. All others are born as a matter of necessity, to work out their karma (the previous actions that brought on the reaction of being born in the material world) and to fulfill their manifold desires, or the sensual "pushings" that keep them bound to repeated birth and death.

As the appearance day of the Supreme Godhead, Janmashtami is for Hindus what Christmas is for Christians, or at least the two are comparable. Unlike the fixed date of Christmas, however, Janmashtami takes place in August or early September, with specifics that vary according to the solar calendar. On the actual day of Janmashtami (also known as Krishnashtami or Gokulashtami), devotees fast until midnight, which is the exact time of the day that Krishna is said to have taken "birth." This fasting is accompanied by a plethora of devotional activities commemorating this most auspicious occasion, and some of these activities are outlined next. .

The *ashtami* part of the name Janmashtami is interesting: The festival occurs on the eighth day (*ashtami*) of a lunar fortnight. That's why it is called "Birth (*janma*) on the eighth day (*ashtami*)," or "Krishna's *ashtami* (eighth day)," or "Gokul (the name of the small town in which he was born) *ashtami*." These *ashtamis*, moreover, are usually celebrated over 2 days. This first day is Krishnashtami or Gokulashtami. The second day is called Janmashtami proper.

Most Janmashtami festivals find devotees cooking at least 108 sumptuous foods for offering to the Lord at midnight, which are then served to anyone in attendance. The number 108 is especially significant here: there are 108 Upanishads, or philosophical Vedic books of learning and, more important, 108 *gopis*, or cowherd devotees of Krishna who assist him in his earthly pastimes. The day will also afford a special viewing of the iconic image of the Lord in the temple, or in one's home, specially decorated and dressed for this exceptional day. In addition, the iconic image will undergo a public bathing ceremony, while priests chant esoteric incantations. The Lord's "body" is bathed with fruit juices and milk products. And then the celebrants take a sip of the mixture with which he was washed, thereby hoping to cleanse away their own sins.

All the while, devotional songs permeate the atmosphere, mingling with the delicious smells of the freshly cooked offerings along with incense and flowers. Sometimes full-length dramas are enacted, detailing the specifics of Krishna's appearance. The performances are drawn from sacred texts, which are also sometimes read aloud for those who congregate to hear them. Or there are traditional Indian style dances specifically created to convey the Lord's pastimes, and there are particular dances that depict his darling birth ceremony.

In addition to these many ways of celebrating Janmashtami, in certain parts of India, most notably in Maharashtra, there is a special ceremony called "Dahi-Handi," which is centered around the breaking of clay pots. In these pots are curd and butter, and they are suspended high above the ground. Young men and children form a human pyramid to reach the pot above them and to break it. The game is meant to evoke thoughts of Krishna's famous pastime of stealing butter from the villagers of Braj—villagers who would in fact purposely leave their dairy products in such pots just to see this charming, endearing boy come and mischievously claim his spoils.

Krishna periodically takes "birth" in other forms, or incarnations, too, but Janmashtami focuses on his appearance in his original two-armed form—the beautiful cowherd boy with luminous dark skin and large, exotic lotus-like eyes. In one of many similar scenes, he runs intensely to catch up to his endearing cows, who playfully charge away from him, just to hear the patter of his little feet galloping after them. When he finally reaches his bovine friends, they lick him excitedly, their affection reaching unknown heights. In the play, his attractive golden garments become slightly undone, and his bewitching earrings dance with a joy of their own. His family and friends lovingly look on, laughing and relishing his every move. The Lord enjoys these bucolic surroundings while playing his flute, surrounded by intimate devotees—the blessed souls in his company know no other picture of beauty and love. Their meditation is complete.

Although he is God, Lord of all, master of the universe, Krishna prefers to spend his time as a simple cowherd boy. For the Hindu, this is quite understandable. Given omnipotence, or the power to do whatever one likes—or to *be* whomever one likes—why wouldn't one adopt the carefree life of an innocent villager, loved by all and with free reign to engage the rural beauties of a special, playful environment? Indeed, this is exactly what God does, say the Vaishnavas, and they long to one day enter into His eternally blissful pastimes of love and devotion. A life well lived, in compliance with Vaishnava religiosity, will in fact garner just this end for the devotee. After death, they will join Krishna in his celestial home, Braj, where they, too, will take part in his mystically resplendent activities, assisting him, loving him, being with him. This truth is the essential religious spirit found in the hearts of devotees on Janmashtami.

Turning to another form of Hinduism, Maha-Shiva-Ratri (also called Shiva Ratri) is the Great Festival of Lord Shiva, an aspect of the Godhead whose focus is universal destruction. The festival is held on the fourteenth day of the dark half of the lunar month of Phalguna, and it is a holiday that is especially important to Shaivites (devotees of Shiva), although it is celebrated by most Hindus.

Much of the festival involves meditation on Shiva, and fasting is an important part of it as well. Shiva is known as the ultimate yogi, or renunciant, so Hindus perform special austerities on this day. Some devotees celebrate by going to Shiva temples, where numerous pilgrims are found offering prayers. The Shiva Linga, or the aniconic form of Shiva, is venerated at temples and in the home, where it is bathed with milk, honey, and water. Specially prepared foods are offered to Shiva, especially *bilva* leaves, fruits, and other edibles that are considered Shiva's favorites. Offering *bilva* leaves on Shiva Ratri is considered particularly pleasing to him. The story is that a hunter once climbed a *bilva* tree to escape the charge of a hungry lion. Not one to be thwarted, the lion sat beneath the tree, waiting for the hunter to fall. As the hunter bided his time in the tree throughout night, he plucked leaves from the *bilva* tree to stay awake. Some of these leaves, which are sacred to Shiva, fell on an idol of Shiva that happened to be at the base of the tree. Shiva, it is said, was pleased by the offering, even though it was unintentional and, because of this, eventually saved the hunter. The event is commemorated on Shiva Ratri by staying up all night and offering *bilva* leaves to Lord Shiva.

Another important aspect of this festival is the incessant chanting of "Om Namo Shivaya Namaha"—"All homage unto Lord Shiva"—which creates a meditative mood in practitioners who chant it with devotion. Attendees also share with each other fabulous retellings of Shiva's many exploits as related in Vedic texts and supplementary literature. A popular one is the "Churning of the Ocean of Milk," which is found in the earliest portions of India's sacred texts. Here, in the process of churning the primordial elements of creation, numerous divine beings inadvertently unearthed a poison that could have destroyed all that is. Shiva, however, would not let this happen.

To save the world, he drank the poison himself, which is why he is often depicted with a blue throat. Although he was powerful enough to accommodate the deadly brew without any severe reactions, he stayed awake for one full night to engage in a healing process. The divine beings who initially took part in the churning helped him get through the night by way of entertainment. They danced for him, sang, displayed various works of art, and performed drama to ease him through his difficult time. These events are commemorated on Shiva Ratri, when Shiva's followers attempt to recreate the Lord's "healing" by "keeping him company throughout the night" and engaging in entertaining activities for his pleasure.

Moving to yet another form of Hinduism, there are numerous festivals and holidays to honor the goddess. The most focused of such holidays occurs every year during the lunar month of Ashwin or Kartik (September–October), when Hindus observe 10 days of ceremonies, rituals, fasts, and feasts glorifying the Supreme Mother of the universe. It begins with the fast of Nava Ratri and ends with holidays known as Dusshera and Vijayadashami.

Despite the many male concepts of divinity in the Hindu tradition, these festivals are devoted solely to the Mother Goddess, known variously as Kali, Durga, Bhavani, Parvati, and so on. The Divine Mother is the personified Energy of the Universe and is an important part of the Hindu paradigm. The title "Durga," which is perhaps the most popular of her names, means "inaccessible," indicating that it is nearly impossible to understand her nature and ontological reality. In addition to her unique personality, she embodies the furious powers of all male divinities, including that of God Himself.

Since the Divine Mother is a manifestation of even the male aspect of the divine, all Hindus celebrate this festival in different ways in different parts of the world, particularly in India. In northern India, for example, the first nine days of the festival, properly called Nava Ratri (nava = nine; ratri = night), is characterized by intense fasting, with complicated procedures gleaned from centuries of tradition. On the tenth day, all fasting comes to an end and celebrations are joyful and lively, including only light feasting, as it is not good to break a fast by gorging oneself on food. In western India, the celebration proceeds a little differently. For the first 9 days, instead of fasting (or, sometimes, in addition to fasting), men, women, and children take part in a special dance ceremony centered on an object of worship, such as an image of Kali or Durga, or a pot or light symbolizing the Goddess. This culminates in a huge feast.

The dancing phenomenon as part of the celebration is especially marked in Gujarat, where a traditional dancing style known as the "Garbha" is favored, with devotees gracefully and, at times, frenetically, moving in circles, usually around a specially decorated pot with a bright lamp smack in the center. The word "Garbha" means "womb," and here the potted lamp is meant to symbolize life within the womb, or more specifically, life in the womb of the Goddess, which is where all living entities must find themselves.

A related dance is known as the "Dandia," in which men and women rhythmically move to devotional music in pairs, holding small, decorated bamboo sticks in their hands; these sticks are called *dandias*. At the very tip of the *dandias* are tiny bells called *ghungroos* that make a festive, jingling sound, especially when the sticks hit each other or various parts of the body. The dance itself is usually backed by complex rhythm and intricate melodies—the music of professionally trained musicians. Those who take part in the dancing begin with slow, methodical movements, gradually increasing with the tempo of the music and eventually giving way to wild dance movements. It becomes quite intense, so much so that each person in the circle not only singles themselves out for a solo performance, spontaneously banging their own sticks on various parts of their body and against their hands; but, often, they madly if playfully run after their partners, threatening to hit them with the sticks as well. This is a tradition that has been part of Goddess festivals for centuries.

In the South, the first 9 days are less intense, but a similar phenomenon occurs. On Dusshera, or the tenth day, an opulent feast is served and a drama of the goddess in action is performed for all who attend. In the eastern part of the country, people focus on the goddess as Durga, with details culled from the ancient Indian histories (the Puranas). They meditate on her, chant her names, and otherwise glorify her with song and dance. "Durga Puja," or the intense worship of the goddess, reaches a noticeable crescendo from the seventh to the tenth day of the festival, with devotees swooning in ecstasy and blissful feasting for one and all.

Most important, on Dusshera, which is the tenth day, as the word suggests, devotees are encouraged to celebrate the triumph of good over evil. On this day, devotees are inclined to remember the defeat and death of the demon king Ravana, who kidnapped Sita—wife of Rama (incarnation of Vishnu, God) and primary manifestation of the Goddess—in the epic known as the Ramayana. Huge effigies of Ravana are burnt in public areas while fireworks and firecrackers loudly proclaim the victory of the righteous.

In northern India, especially, Dusshera is celebrated in conjunction with Rama-lila or Rama's Spiritual Drama, traditional plays in which scenes from the epic saga, depicting the famous Rama-Ravana battle are enacted by professional acting troupes. Even here, the festival still carries the flavor of the goddess, however, for the story is really about Sita's, or the goddess's, victory over evil. Like all other Hindu holidays, we are here reminded that we, too, must be victorious over the darker side of life and rejoice in the glory of God.

NOTES

1. "Festivals" in John Bowker, ed., *Oxford Concise Dictionary of World Religions* (New York: United Press, 2000), p. 193.

2. Much of this information is from the "Hindu calendar" found on the Wikipedia, http://en.wikipedia.org/wiki/Hindu_calendar. See also "Calendars Through the Ages" at http://webexhibits.org/calendars/calendar-indian.html.

3. Ibid.

4. Ibid.

5. For more on fasting and its significance in Hindu tradition, see Bhrigu-muni Dasa, *Dearest to Visnu: Ekadasi and Dvadasi According to the Hari-Bhakti-Vilasa* (Helsinki, Finland: Absolute Truth Press, 2001) and Krsna Balaram Swami, *Ekadasi: The Day of Lord Hari* (San Francisco, CA: The Bhaktivedanta Institute, 1986).

6

MAJOR FIGURES

Hinduism is best understood by looking at the lives of those who practice it. Unlike other world religions, Hindu theological systems consider certain historical figures to be God, or incarnations of God, and several of these are considered here. Along with such divine personalities, the biographical profiles in this section highlight specially empowered beings and still others who are merely great saints. Finally, some of the biographical sketches are of extraordinary men and women, who gave their lives for a higher cause. An attempt is made to present these pivotal Hindu personalities in chronological order, although because of the uncertainty of their dates, this may not always be possible. Bolded names refer to other biographical profiles found in this chapter.

Vyasa (ca. 5,000 years ago)

Veda Vyasa was the legendary compiler of the Vedic literature, India's most ancient sacred texts. Considered the "literary incarnation of Vishnu (God)," Vyasa is said to have not only divided the one Veda into four separate books (hence his name Vyasa, which means "divider," or "editor"), but is also said to have compiled the Mahabharata, the Puranas, and many other revered books in the Hindu corpus of literature.

He is known as Krishna Dvaipayana ("the dark one who was born on an island"), which refers to his mysterious birth as portrayed in the Mahabharata, and in modern Indian languages he is known simply as Vyasa. Whatever one calls him, he is deemed to be the ideal sage, omniscient, truthful, purest of the pure, and possessor of essential knowledge.

It is said that he dictated the Vedic literature while the elephant-headed Ganesh actually did the writing. Vyasa's plan was to consolidate Vedic knowledge and make it accessible for people in the modern era, whom he described as unfortunate, short-lived, and full of faults. In addition, he felt the need to put Vedic knowledge into writing because people of this age could not memorize the texts after hearing them only once, as Vedic adepts had done in ages gone by. All Hindu knowledge is gauged against Vyasa's Vedic literature.

Andal Alvar (ca. ninth century C.E.)

Andal Alvar was part of a group of "God-intoxicated" individuals known as the Alvars (literally, "immersed in God"), 12 poet-saints who wrote beautiful devotional poetry and who lived their lives in complete dedication and surrender. Their focus was the Supreme Soul as Krishna, the beautiful dark-eyed Lord, mysterious and alluring. The earthly sojourn of the Alvars ranges from the seventh century C.E. to the tenth century C.E., with Andal's father (also an Alvar) clearly being in the early ninth century.

One day Perialvar, as her father was known, was working in a garden of basil (*tulasi*), a plant that is very dear to Krishna, the Supreme Lord. Just then, he noticed a baby girl. The childless Perialvar accepted the child as a gift from God, and named her Goda, "born of Mother Earth."

Her father raised her as a devotee of Krishna, and from a very early age she decided that she wanted to "marry" Lord Ranganath, the deity or iconic image of Krishna that appears in one of India's most famous temples, Sri Rangam. Her spiritual marriage with God began to vex her father, who naturally wanted a normal life for her. Realizing her purity of purpose, however, he gave her the name Andal, "she who rules the Lord," for in her intense desire she had attained a closeness with God that few will ever achieve.

Her poems, the "Tiruppavai" and the "Nachiyar Tirumoli," are said to represent the highest level of devotional fervor, and they are still sung daily in every south Indian Vaishnava shrine dedicated to Krishna. Her life epitomizes divine bridal longing, complete and without distraction. It is said that she achieved her goal and, indeed, that God is her husband.[1]

Shankara (ca. 788–820 C.E.)

Also known as Adi Shankara and as Shankara Acharya, Shankara was among the most important Indian philosophers and reformers and the founder of the Advaita, or non-dual, school of Hindu philosophy. He taught that "all is one" and that everyone and everything is in essence God. Widely regarded as an incarnation of Lord Shiva—God in His aspect as the Destroyer of the Universe—Shankara's devotees tend to emphasize the divinity of the Shiva aspect of the Godhead and advocate merging with the Supreme at the time of death. They also honor all aspects of Hindu divinity, seeing the gods as different and yet as one and the same.

Born of Brahman parents in southern India, his superior intellectual powers were soon apparent as he mastered a wide range of religious and philosophical texts at a very early age. He synthesized the immensely diverse spectrum of Hindu philosophical and theistic thought into a single coherent system. This he did by promoting what was eventually called "Smartism," which is a philosophy that honors all aspects of the Godhead. He was committed to the original Veda—India's most ancient religious literature, but he gave it an impersonalistic spin. This he did to take specifics away from the Deity, thus allowing the synthesis he was determined to achieve.

In Shankara's time, Hinduism and its attendant Vedic literature had lost a large following because of the influence of Buddhism and Jainism, two heterodox traditions that were based on nontheistic principles of virtue and psychological empowerment. Shankara reestablished the importance of the Vedas, allowing Hinduism to regain strength and popularity. He naturally tailored his Vedic teaching for his audience of Buddhists and Jains, however, and later Vaishnava reformers take him to task for this. Even though he lived for only 32 years, his impact on India and on Hinduism is formidable, and his followers still study his works and abide by his teachings.

Ramanuja (1017–1137)

Ramanuja, alternately called Ramanujacharya, was a preeminent Hindu theologian born in Sri Perumbudur, South India. He wrote many works glorifying Vishnu, God, using both philosophy and poetry. An exponent of a sort of "qualified non-dualism," wherein he acknowledged humankind's oneness with its Creator but detected a difference as well, he is considered one of India's earliest systematic monotheistic thinkers. He taught that living beings are one with God in quality but that they are different in terms of quantity. For example, both are essentially spirit as opposed to matter, and they possess certain universal characteristics such as strength, beauty, wealth, fame, and knowledge. And yet God is great, or exhibits these qualities in full, whereas humans (and all other living entities, too) are small, with only partial access to these qualities. This, according to Ramanuja, is the distinction between God and His children.

Ramanuja had many distinguished predecessors in his lineage. Natamuni and Yamuna are perhaps the most well known, for they were luminaries who contributed numerous written tomes and their lives were examples of superlative devotion. There were also the 12 "Alvars," a loosely knit confederation of poet-saints, whose lives and collected works are the main inspiration for his line of thinking.

He died at Srirangam, a famous pilgrimage center in the south, where his lineage, the Sri Sampradaya, continues to thrive.[2]

Madhva (1238–1317)

Also known as Madhva Acharya, Ananda Tirtha, and Purnaprajna, Madhva was one of India's greatest theologians. He is the systematizer of "Dvaita" philosophy—which is the idea of "two-ness," that is, that God and the living entity are eternally distinct. The two are never one. This idea, couched in the most sophisticated theological jargon, is Madhva's most memorable and noteworthy contribution to the world, defying the "oneness" doctrine of Shankara and others, who claimed that "oneness with God" is the greatest achievement in self-realization.

The little that is known of Madhva's personal life is largely derived from the Madhva-vijaya, a work by Narayana Bhatta, the son of a direct disciple of Madhva. According to this work, Madhva was born of Tulu-speaking parents in the Karnataka region of South India. It says that he is an incarnation of the wind-god, and that he descends into this mortal world in three successive incarnations. First he appears as Hanuman, the half-monkey and half-man follower of Lord Rama, the incarnation of God described in the epic text known as the Ramayana; then he appears as Bhimasena, one of the Pandava brothers (the heroes of the epic narrative, the Mahabharata); and finally he comes as Madhva, who in the current age descends to rectify the philosophical misconceptions of his predecessors.

During his lifetime, Madhva wrote important commentaries on Hinduism's many sacred texts, including the Upanishads, Bhagavad Gita, Brahma Sutras, Mahabharata, and the Bhagavata Purana. In addition, he wrote many original works that dealt with important aspects of his "two-ness" doctrine. His final years were spent in teaching, meditation, and worship.

In the end he instructed his followers not to sit still or to even focus on their own salvation, but to go forth and to share with others what they have realized.[3]

Vallabhacharya (1479–1531)

Vallabha, as he is also known, was one of the important religious reformers of sixteenth-century India. He taught the importance of loving Krishna. His followers particularly emphasize God as "Bala Krishna," or Krishna in the form of a lovable child. A paternal mood thus engulfs many of his followers, and their theology is crafted around this kind of nurturing sensibility. Vallabha himself showed devotion to the deity or image of Krishna known as Sri Nathaji, which is the boy Krishna who lifts Mount Govardhana, protecting his devotees by using the hill as an umbrella to block the terrible rains sent by one of the Lord's adversaries.

Vallabha's system of philosophy is called "pure non-dualism"; it is pure in the sense that it is "undefiled by *maya,* or illusion." The implication here is that non-dualism, as commonly understood, is the product of the illusory energy. Oneness with God, says Vallabha, must be understood in perspective—that living beings are one with Him in spiritual quality, but not in spiritual quantity—He is great and ordinary living beings are small. Vallabha's religious lineage is known as the Rudra Sampradaya of Vaisnavism and also as Pushtimarga, or "the path of grace."

His youth was spent in Benares, where he learned philosophy and became a master in all the Hindu scriptures. Later, he relocated to Adail, near modern Allahabad and settled down to married life. His devotion is the stuff of legends, and his original works and commentaries on sacred texts are studied to this day. After his demise, the lineage was largely in the hands of his son, Vitthalnath (1516–1586), who elaborated on temple ritual and systematized Vallabha's teaching.[4]

Chaitanya Mahaprabhu (1486–1534)

Accepted by his followers as Krishna and Radha (both male and female aspects of the Supreme Lord) in one body, or as God in the guise of his own devotee, Mahaprabhu is considered the preeminent ecstatic mystic of medieval India, particularly of Bengal. His life story illustrates numerous superlative examples—that of a religious scholar, a householder (married) devotee, a social reformer, a renounced monk, and, finally, a lover of God.

His short life of 48 years began when he was called to earth by Advaita Acharya, an important senior devotee of the period, viewed by the tradition as an incarnation of Maha-Vishnu, the Lord of Creation Himself. At birth, Mahaprabhu was given the name Vishvambhara ("One who sustains the universe"). His nickname was Nimai, for he was born under a *neem* tree. The darling of the neighborhood, he was adored by all of the local women, much as the women of Braj had adored Krishna, 4,500 years earlier. He was precocious like Krishna, too, and became a scholar at an early age. Whereas, initially, he used this scholarship to vex the devotees, taunting them by quoting obscure Vedic texts that seemed to contradict their devotional conclusions, after a pivotal meeting with Ishvara Puri, a sage who initiated him into the chanting of the holy name, he used this

Chaitanya Mahaprabhu (1486–1533), the combined golden form of Radha and Krishna, and the teacher of chanting God's names as a yogic science. Courtesy of Per Sinclair.

same knowledge to defeat all opposing views. He became the champion of Krishna devotion and created a revolution in consciousness that is still felt throughout the subcontinent and around the world.

The paradigmatic devotee, Chaitanya Mahaprabhu is one of India's most renowned proponents of loving devotion, Bhakti-yoga, in which God is approached through joyful celebratory activities, such as song and dance. In fact, he is particularly remembered for emphasizing the chanting of God's holy names—usually in the form of "the Great Chant for Deliverance," Hare Krishna, Hare Krishna, Krishna Krishna, Hare Hare / Hare Rama, Hare Rama, Rama Rama, Hare Hare—as the most effective yogic process for the current day and age. He and his scholarly followers delineated a great science for singing God's glories in which one's heartfelt prayers are augmented by tangible procedures for attaining lofty spiritual goals. In the twentieth century, the teachings of Chaitanya Mahaprabhu were brought to the West by A. C. Bhaktivedanta Swami Prabhupada, a representative of the Gaudiya Matha branch of Chaitanya's tradition.[5]

Rupa Goswami (1489–1564)

Rupa Goswami is perhaps the most respected Vaishnava theologian, poet, and dramatist in the lineage of Sri Chaitanya. As such, he is the devotee of Krishna par excellence. He is known as one of the Six Goswamis of Vrindavan, and, along with his nephew, Jiva Goswami, is considered primary among India's preeminent religious philosophers.

Chaitanya himself—whose life was a virtual embodiment of spiritual ecstasy—left no writing of his own (except his very famous eight verses). Instead, he gave the task of systematizing his teachings to the Six Goswamis, particularly to Rupa.

Although belonging to Karnataka Brahmin ancestry in South India, the family of Rupa Goswami migrated to Bengal near the end of the fourteenth century. He was employed by the then Muslim Emperor of Bengal, Nawab Husein Shah, and was known by the name Sakara Malik. Although working for the Muslim leader of Bengal, Sri Rupa never forgot his intense devotion for Krishna. The name Rupa Goswami was subsequently given to him by Sri Chaitanya.

Rupa Goswami's elaborate science of devotional yogic practice was outlined in his numerous scholarly works, particularly in the Bhakti-rasamrta-sindhu and the Ujjvala-nilamani. In these two mammoth tomes, he described religious sentiments in elaborate categories, as well as methodical procedures for imbibing these sentiments. His poetic system of devotional service to Krishna, the Supreme Godhead, has been described as "the science of love," for he outlined a nonsectarian method by which one can gently place oneself into the heart of the Lord. Each person, teaches Rupa, can enter into the pastimes of God by hearing and chanting, and by remembering his otherworldly activities under the guidance of a pure devotee, a doctor of the soul.[6]

Jahnava Devi (ca. sixteenth century)

Jahnava Devi is remembered as the leader of the Chaitanya Vaishnava community in late sixteenth-century Bengal. The wife of Chaitanya's chief associate, Nityananda, she was widowed when still fairly young. Her sister, Vasudha, had two children, and she raised them—Ganga, a girl, and Virabhadra, a boy—and adopted a little boy named Ramachandra as well. The three youngsters also became leading Vaishnava devotees in their time.

History relates that Jahnava won the highest level of respect throughout the Vaishnava community. She was known by all as Ishvari, the feminine form of the commonly used word for God (Ishvara). At the very least, the term indicates the great respect that others had for her. At best, it was recognition of her divinity; Nityananda was seen as an incarnation of Balarama, Krishna's elder brother. As his wife, she was envisioned as the Divine Energy of the Lord, or God in His female feature.

Evidence of her divinity is recounted in several sacred texts of the period, especially in the Nityananda Vamsavistara. In one such account, Virabhadra, her stepson, was looking for a teacher, someone to guide him in spiritual life, but he wanted only the topmost Vaishnava to be his guru. One day, he saw Jahnava as she was completing her bath. While she was drying her hair, her wet cloth slipped down. To conceal her naked body, she manifested two extra arms to hold up the falling cloth. Virabhadra was impressed by this show of divinity, for only manifestations of Vishnu, or God, and his closest associates are said to have four-armed forms, and he asked her to initiate him.

Perhaps Jahnava's most significant contribution was to address the theological sophistication of the growing Chaitanya Vaishnava movement. At the famous Kheturi festival, convened to systematize the doctrines and beliefs of the newly formed Vaishnava community in Bengal, she played the role of religious authority, lending approval to innovations in practices and to the then recent theological formulations on the nature of Chaitanya and his incarnation. Her statements were accepted as truth, indicating how revered she was by the Vaishnava community.

Sur Das (ca. sixteenth century)

Sur Das was a prolific composer, saint, and poet. He is primarily known for his Sur Sagara (Sur's Ocean), a magnum opus of devotional poetry that is arguably the most beautiful India has ever produced. Its focus is Krishna, Sur's beautiful dark-eyed Lord, but includes interesting descriptions of Radha's love as well.

A congenitally blind bard, Sur Das composed poetry in the Braj-Bhasha, a dialect of Hindi peculiar to the Braja region of Uttar Pradesh.

The philosophical perspectives and theological moods of Sur Das's work clearly reflect the times in which he lived. He was very much a part of the "Bhakti" movement—or the trend toward personalistic theism, characterized by loving attitudes and devotional expressions toward the Divine—that was sweeping India in the sixteenth century. This movement represented a move away from the rigid intellectualism of former days, forging a grassroots spiritual revival and garnering empowerment for the common people. No longer were theological subjects the monopoly of the Brahmins or the intellectual elite. Sur Das and others like him saw devotional sentiments literally taken into the streets, where singing and dancing in glorification of the supreme became the most effective and popular form of communing with God.[7]

Tulsidas (1532–1623)

Born in Rajpur, India, in the district of Banda in Uttar Pradesh, Tulsidas was a medieval Hindi poet and philosopher. He is famous for having written 12 books and is sometimes regarded as an incarnation of Valmiki, the author of the Ramayana (the sacred scripture about Rama, the incarnation of Vishnu). He is identified with Valmiki because his most famous work is the Ramcharitmanas ("The Lake that is the Story of Rama"), which is a Hindi reworking of Valmiki's classic. Most Hindu families, unable to read Valmiki's Sanskrit original, only know the Ramayana through Tulsidas's regional version, which includes some imaginative elaboration and philosophical variation.

Mirabai (ca. late sixteenth century)

Mirabai is among the most famous devotional poets of north India. The only daughter of a prince named Ratan Singh, owner of a fortress-city founded by her grandfather, Mirabai is said to have been devoted to Krishna, the beautiful dark-eyed Lord, from a very early age. Her father was often traveling, engaging in his princely duties, so she was raised at her grandfather's house, and on his death, her uncle Viram Dev became her sole guardian. It was he who married her to Bhoja Raj, the heir apparent to the throne of the famous warrior, Rana Sanga.

Mirabai took no interest in her earthly spouse, bearing him no children (a tragedy in the India of her time), because she believed herself to be married to Krishna, her Lord. She saw only God as her husband. As she grew in years, so, too, did she grow detached from the affairs of the world and from her obligations to her family. She began to practically live at the temple, where she prayed with great intensity, conversed with saintly people of the period, and joyfully danced before the image of Krishna with wild abandon. Her corpus of mellifluent poetry and her impassioned cry for her divine cowherd lover still resound throughout the subcontinent.[8]

Ram Mohan Roy (1772–1833)

Ram Mohan Roy was the founder of the Brahmo Samaj, one of the first Hindu reform movements in modern India. His name is especially associated with the abolition of *sati* (the custom in which a widow, in deference to her husband, will throw herself on his funeral pyre). Ram Mohan is also famous for speaking out against polygamy, which was prevalent in his day. He showed that it was, in fact, contrary to Hindu law.

By way of the social, legal, and religious reforms that instigated the Brahmo Samaj, he was especially interested in humanism and the needs of his people. His emphasis, he assured his audience, was not to break away from authentic Hindu traditions, but only to deny speculative innovations that were added later. He wanted to take the original religion of the Hindus and restore it to its original purity, although his primary concern was to do this in a way that would best serve the people of his day. He was more people-centered than God-centered. Accordingly, he insisted on the authority of the Vedas and the Upanishads, the authorized texts of ancient Hindu culture. However, he condemned idolatry and other common Hindu practices that he deemed of later origin.

In 1831, he traveled to Great Britain and elsewhere in Europe as an ambassador of Hindu culture. Not long after his death, his brainchild, the Brahmo Samaj, divided into two groups because of the differing emphasis of its leaders. Debendranath Tagore became the leader of the Adi Brahmo Samaj and Keshub Chandra Sen of the Brahmo Samaj of India. Both groups have diminished in the modern period. Even so, the Brahmo Samaj is remembered as a pioneer of the Hindu renaissance.[9]

Swaminarayan (1781–1830)

Swami Sahajananda founded a religious community at age 21. He later became known as Swaminarayan, after the incantation, or *mantra*, that he taught to his followers. ("Swaminarayan" refers to the Supreme Controller, Narayana—another name for Vishnu, or God.) The Swaminarayan lineage is thus part of the Vaishnava tradition—as it promotes the worship of Vishnu—and focuses its endeavors on salvation through total submission or devotion—*bhakti*—to the Supreme Godhead.

Given the name Ghanashyam at birth, Sahajananda was born in the village of Chapiya, near Ayodhya, North India. Developing expertise in the scriptures by the age of 7, he renounced home as a young boy and proceeded to spend almost 10 years on a spiritual pilgrimage across the entire subcontinent. Settling in Gujarat, he spent the next three decades formulating a sociospiritual revolution. These are the beginnings of his lineage, dedicated to social reform, serving the poor and the needy, challenging myth and superstition, and tending to addictions and blind faith.

Today the Swaminarayan lineage represents a particularly powerful form of Hinduism, with a growing number of followers worldwide. Some Hindus worship Swaminarayan as the ninth incarnation of Vishnu, the Oversoul of the Universe.[10]

Dayananda Sarasvati (1824–1883)

Born in Gujarat, India, Dayananda Sarasvati is remembered as the founder of the Arya Samaj, a Hindu reform movement founded in 1875. His teachings promote the infallibility of the Vedas, India's ancient texts of knowledge, and he emphasized the doctrines of karma (causation) and rebirth (reincarnation). He also wrote much about the importance of monasticism, such as celibate student life and that of a mature renunciant.

Dayananda Sarasvati, unlike Ram Mohan Roy, the founder of India's other great reform movement, the Brahmo Samaj, did not borrow concepts from other religions. In fact, he is known for his criticism of Islam and Christianity, in particular. He saw encroaching faiths from other lands as contributing to the corruption of India's own pure faith of Hinduism.

While endorsing traditional values and standards of religion, the Arya Samaj unequivocally condemned idolatry, animal sacrifice, ancestor worship, pilgrimage, offerings made in temples, the caste system, untouchability—practices and characteristics of long-standing Hindu tradition. The argument was that although these may have for many centuries been an accepted part of what is today known as Hinduism, they were not sanctioned by the original Vedas and should therefore be excised from Hindu tradition.[11]

Helena Petrovna Blavatsky (1831–1891)

Although not born in India, Blavatsky is important to modern-day Hinduism for numerous reasons. Originally hailing from the Russian Ukraine, she married the much older N. V. Blavatsky, but rather than forging ahead with connubial bliss, she quickly embarked on more than two decades of extensive travel, bringing her into contact with mystic traditions from around the world.

In 1873, Madame Blavatsky, as she came to be called, arrived in New York. In July 1875, she established a "philosophico-religious society," and in the fall of the same year, she became the principal founder, along with Henry Steel Olcott and William Q. Judge of the Theosophical Society, a movement founded on the principles of Perennial Wisdom, with an emphasis on the traditions associated with Hinduism.

She devoted the remainder of her life to the movement's humanitarian and educational goals. Her spiritual insights are revealed in her first major work, *Isis Unveiled,* and in the pages of *The Theosophist,* a magazine that she founded and edited. Eventually, she and Olcott established a major headquarters for the Theosophical Society in India. In 1887, she settled in London, initiating a new magazine and also writing her magnum opus, entitled *The Secret Doctrine,* which was published in 1888. She and W. Q. Judge also formed the Esoteric Section of the Theosophical Society and soon afterward she wrote other esoteric works exploring an inner vision of Hindu wisdom.

Sri Ramakrishna (1836–1886)

Sri Ramakrishna taught that God can be experienced as directly as we experience the day-to-day world, only more intensely, and that all religions are ultimately one in that they are all paths to the same God.

Born in a small village 60 miles north of Calcutta, his birth name was Gadadhar; his family name was Chatterjee. From his earliest youth, he was given to mystical experiences and religious fervor. In 1852, as a teenager, he relocated in Calcutta to work with his brother, hoping to support the larger family who stayed back in the village.

In Calcutta he soon became a priest in the famous Kali Temple at Dakeshineshwar, which was a village a few miles to the north. Here he began the spiritual practices of austerity and deep meditation for which he would eventually become so famous. Although his spiritual discipline and its ensuing perspective were broad-based, the Goddess Kali—the Divine Mother of the Universe—would predominate his religious worldview forevermore. His intense practices, in fact, awarded him visions of the Goddess in due course, although his family thought him merely eccentric. Fearing for his sanity, they persuaded him to return to their village, hoping that a normal life, with marriage to a lovely young girl, would bring him to his senses.

The girl, from a neighboring village, was Sarada Devi—a great spiritualist in her own right. With a marriage that exacerbated his spiritual longing, then, he returned to the Kali Temple and became even more immersed in his spiritual practices.

In 1861, he discovered Tantric practices—or mystic, psychosexual dimensions of spirituality—and quickly achieved results that most people take a lifetime to procure. He also learned Advaita Vedanta, or the impersonal reality of God's formless nature, under the tutelage of an itinerant monk named Tota Puri. As a result, he soon experienced a high level of impersonal realization; however, his thirst for spiritual experience did not end there. He practiced Sufism (mystic branch of Islam) under an adept named Govinda Roy and also experienced visions of Jesus and the Virgin Mary after throwing himself into the study of Christianity. All of this was to lead to his pluralistic conception of religion, which he taught his followers.

Gradually, numerous students came to him for spiritual instruction, and, among themselves, they chose Swami Vivekananda to lead them. Toward the end, Ramakrishna was concerned that his students learn as much as they could from him, and from his student, for he knew he was dying of throat cancer.[12]

Bhaktivinoda Thakur (1838–1914)

Born of a wealthy family of landowners, Kedarnath Datta, as Bhakti-vinoda was known in his youth, grew up in a traditional Hindu household of rural Bengal. The family were Shakta Hindus; that is, they worshiped the Mother Goddess, as is common in that part of the country. The title "Bhak-tivinoda," "one who takes pleasure in devotion to God," was conferred on Kedarnath Datta in 1886 in recognition of his prominence as a Vaishnava theologian, specifically regarding the worship of Krishna, the personality of Godhead. But he was not always interested in Vaishnavism.

As a young boy, he was more interested in family and work, both by necessity and inclination. When he was 14 years old, he left his natal home and moved to Calcutta with his uncle Kashi Prashad Ghosh, a well-known patriot and author. Soon after, Bhaktivinoda attended Hindu College in Calcutta, where he developed close relationships with such noteworthy personalities as Ishwar Chandra Vidyasagar, his college teacher and lifelong friend; Keshub Chandra Sen, a classmate; Michael Madhusudan Datta, a literary associate who was predisposed to Christianity; Bankim Chandra Chatterjee, a civil service colleague and eminent novelist; and Sisir Kumar Ghosh, a prominent newspaper publisher and author. All of these men distinguished themselves in nineteenth-century Bengal.

Significantly, while at Hindu College, Bhaktivinoda received a Western education and was exposed to European culture. These are assets he would draw on in his later career as a writer of theological treatises. While in school he developed an interest in American Unitarianism and became enamored by Western philosophers. By the time he was 18 years old, he left the city and relocated in rural Orissa, where he secured a government job with the British in the judicial service. For the next 25 years, he was employed as a civil servant and worked his was up to the honored position of district magistrate.

During these years, he had 14 children, all of whom eventually developed an interest in philosophy and religion, for this became a major preoccupation for their father. When he was 29 years old, Bhaktivinoda became a follower of Chaitanya Mahaprabhu (1486–1533), the religious ecstatic associated with the heart of Bengal Vaishnavism, or Krishna worship, and eventually a leader within the Chaitanya Vaishnava movement. Once adopting the tradition as his own, taking initiation from the sage Vipin Vihari Goswami when he was 42 years old, Bhaktivinoda became its most outspoken representative, contributing greatly to the furtherance of Vaish-

Bhaktisiddhanta Sarasvati Thakur. The
highly intellectual and revolutionary Vaishnava reformer. He was the spiritual master
of His Divine Grace A.C. Bhaktivedanta
Swami Prabhupada, the founder and spiritual preceptor of the International Society for Krishna Consciousness (ISKCON).
Courtesy of Per Sinclair.

nava philosophy, theology, and literature. He edited and published more
than 100 books on these subjects in Sanskrit, Bengali, and English, including an autobiography entitled Svalikhita Jivani (1896). His work includes
translations of sacred texts, original philosophy, comparative religion, and
theologically rooted novels and poetry.

As early as 1880, he sent copies of his works to Ralph Waldo Emerson
in the United States in an attempt to export the teaching of Chaitanya's
Vaishnavism to the West. By 1896, some of Bhaktivinoda's English writings arrived in Canada, Great Britain, and Australia, presaging the work of
his son, Bhaktisiddhanta Sarasvati and his son's illustrious disciple, A.C.
Bhaktivedanta Swami Prabhupada.[13]

Annie Besant (1847–1933)

Like Helena Petrovna (Madame) Blavatsky, with whom she is closely related, Annie Besant was not born in India. Originally, she was Annie Wood
of Clapham, London. An uneventful youth led to her marriage in 1867 to
Frank Besant, who became a vicar in Lincolnshire. Although her marriage
resulted in the happy birth of two children, it was nonetheless beleaguered
by problems. Besant was disinterested in the shallow Christianity of her
day—the Christianity of her husband—and, for a time, became an athe-
ist. Her increasingly irreligious views led to a legal separation in 1873. The
courts awarded the children to their father because of Besant's unconven-
tional views.

At this point, she had become a member of the National Secular Society, which preached "free thought." She was also part of the Fabian Society, a socialist organization whose members included playwright George
Bernard Shaw. At this point in her life, social and political reform seems
to have satisfied her hunger for some higher truth, replacing the stilted
religion of her younger days.

In time, however, she became interested in theosophy as a way of know-
ing God. Once converted her enthusiasm could not be contained. She was
not merely a member—she quickly became a leader of the Theosophical
Society, helping to spread theosophical beliefs around the world, especially in India. Making the subcontinent her home, she became involved
in Indian nationalism and, in 1916, established the Indian Home Rule
League of which she became president. Her longtime interest in education had earlier resulted in the founding of the Central Hindu College at
Benares.

She is perhaps most readily remembered for her books, especially *Esoteric Christianity* (1902), and in relation to Jiddu Krishnamurti (whom she
promoted as "the new messiah" and as an incarnation of the Buddha). This
began in the late 1920s, when she traveled to England and the United States
with him on a promotional campaign hoping to change the world. Eventually, sometime in 1929, Krishnamurti rejected these claims, much to her
embarrassment. In the end, she was reunited with her own children and
died in India, where she is remembered as an extraordinary personality.

Sri Sarada Devi (1853–1920)

For many Hindus, the affectionate term *Holy Mother* refers to Sarada
Devi, Ramakrishna's wife and feminine counterpart. According to tradi-

tional Indian custom, she was betrothed to him while still a child. Years later, at the age of 18, she left her parental home to live with him, although he was located near Calcutta, 60 miles away from everything she held dear. Still, she came to him not merely as a wife but as a spiritual seeker who recognized his unique status as a teacher. Thus, she approached him as his first disciple.

Sarada Devi was a spiritual luminary in her own way, and yet she served Ramakrishna and his disciples as a humble servant for many years. After Ramakrishna died, she carried on his religious ministry, serving as guide and inspiration for the fledgling spiritual movement.

The example set by Sarada Devi for Ramakrishna's followers, as an ideal disciple, nun, wife, teacher, and especially mother, who took great care of her many spiritual children—his other followers—will be remembered for centuries to come. Those who associated with her were overwhelmed by her spirit of love and selfless service. She accepted them all as her children, irrespective of nationality, religious affiliation, or social position. She turned no one away. Her love seemed all-encompassing.

Rabindranath Tagore (1861–1941)

Regarded as one of the most important writers in modern Indian literature, Tagore was awarded knighthood in 1915. He subsequently relinquished this honor, however, as a protest against the Massacre of Amritsar, where British troops killed 400 Indian demonstrators protesting colonial laws. A Bengali poet, novelist, and educator, he won the Nobel Prize for Literature in 1913.

Rabindranath was born in Calcutta in a wealthy and prominent Brahmin family. His father's name was Maharishi Debendranath Tagore, his mother's was Sarada Devi (not to be confused with Ramakrishna's wife). The youngest child in the family, he started to compose poems at the age of 8. As a youth he went to the Bengal Academy where he studied Bengali history and culture and then to University College, London, where he studied law. He left after a year without completing his studies.

Among his other accomplishments, Tagore founded a school outside Calcutta, Visva-Bharati, which was dedicated to both Western and Indian philosophy and education. It became a university in 1921. Although known in India from early on, Tagore gained a reputation as a writer in the United States and in England after the publication of *Gitanjali: Song Offerings*, in which he explores the themes of both divine and human love.[14]

Swami Vivekananda (1863–1902)

Although virtually unknown before 1893's American Parliament of Religions Conference, at which he represented Hinduism, Vivekananda is the Hindu most responsible for the modern West's perception of the religion. A disciple of Ramakrishna, he sought to convey the rational and humanistic side of Hindu philosophy. He was chiefly concerned with creating a synthesis of East and West, of religion and science. His theological stance, like that of his teacher, was the impersonalistic view of the Divine, the oneness of all existence. Unlike his teacher, however, he deemphasized the theistic notion of the Goddess, preferring instead to stay in the realm of abstract philosophy.

A philanthropist with a Hindu bent, he emphasized service to humanity as among the best approaches to realizing one's unity with the Supreme. He is said to have had, like his master, direct, intuitive experience of ultimate reality. In the course of a short life of 39 years, of which only one decade was devoted to his public ministry, he contributed a number of now-classic treatises on Hindu philosophy. In addition, he delivered what seemed like countless lectures, wrote countless letters to his many friends and disciples, composed a collection of poems, and acted as spiritual guide to the many spiritual seekers who came to him for instruction. He also organized the Ramakrishna Order of monks, which is one of the most perseverant religious institutions of modern India. It is dedicated to the propagation of Hindu spirituality not only in India but also in the United States and other parts of the world.[15]

Sister Nivedita (1867–1911)

Born in Dungannon, Ireland, Margaret Noble, as she was known in her youth, belonged to a family of Irish freedom fighters. Initially a school teacher, she eventually happened on the path of Swami Vivekananda, just after his appearance at the 1893 Parliament of the World's Religions at Chicago. Five years later, she found herself traveling with him to India. There, in 1898, she was initiated and given the name Nivedita, which means, "the dedicated one."

Appalled by India's poverty and disease, she sought to awaken the Hindu nation to the corruption and abusiveness of British rule, which she blamed for the deplorable condition of the people. She championed the cause of women's education and, with the cooperation of Mother Sarada Devi, the wife of Ramakrishna, opened a school for girls in Calcutta in 1898. She worked tirelessly for the cause of the Ramakrishna Mission and even went with Vivekananda to England and elsewhere on a preaching mission and to raise money for her school. She met with philosopher and patriot Sri Aurobindo and other national leaders to better India's condition.

Her health was eventually affected by her rigorous activities. Perceiving that her end was near, she wrote her will and left her possessions to the Ramakrishna Mission to be used for her school. To end her life, she chanted the famous verse of the Upanishads, "Lead us from the unreal to the Real. Lead us from darkness to Light. Lead us from death to Immortality." Today, in Darjeeling, a memorial is inscribed with these words: "Here repose the ashes of Sister Nivedita, who gave her all to India."

Mohandas (Mahatma) Gandhi (1869–1948)

Mohandas Karamchand Gandhi is considered one of the greatest national leaders of the twentieth century, if not of all time. So loved is he in India that he is often considered "the father of the nation." His perceptions and formulas for nonviolent action, or civil disobedience, brought his own country to independence and influenced many other world leaders, including Martin Luther King, Jr.

Born in Porbandar, India, which is on the west coast of Gujarat, Gandhi hailed from a rich, influential family of the time. He was from the merchant caste. Although his ancestors were largely Vallabhite Vaishnavas, or worshippers of Krishna, the deity most associated with monotheism in India, his mother leaned toward Jainism, a nontheistic religion that emphasizes nonviolence and vegetarianism. These religious leanings would inform most of Gandhi's future philosophy and practice.

In fact, Gandhi claimed that he was most influenced by his mother, whose life was an endless chain of fasts and vows. When, as an adolescent, he secretly smoked, ate meat, told lies, or wore Western clothing, all of which were anathema in his traditional Hindu household, he suffered intense feelings of guilt. He later wrote that these initial feelings were the source of his firm resolutions about moral behavior, feelings that would not only define the balance of his life but also make him noteworthy in the history of humankind.

As a young man he went to London to study law and eventually practiced in Bombay. Wanting to expand his influence, he decided to move his practice to where people needed him most. From 1893 to 1914, he worked for an Indian law firm in South Africa. During these years Gandhi suffered humiliating experiences rooted in racial discrimination, leading him to protest on behalf of the Indian community in South Africa.

His name became synonymous with such protest campaigns, and, as a result of these experiences, he gradually developed his own unique form of nonviolent resistance. His method became known as Satyagraha (literally, "truth-force"). This consisted of sending hordes of passive resisters, often women, directly into the precincts of their oppressors. They would then nonviolently allow themselves to receive the blows of those who opposed them. The net result was that the deliverers of these blows would eventually become sickened by their own cruel behavior, creating in them a sense of sympathy they had not previously experienced. As history relates, Gandhi's methods were largely successful.

Returning to India in January 1915, he soon became a dominant figure in the Indian National Congress Party, which was based on a policy of non-cooperation with the British. Although total noncooperation was eventually deemed impractical, Gandhi continued his tactic of civil disobedience, organizing protest marches against unpopular British measures, such as an irrational "salt tax," and he boycotted British goods. Because of such rebellious actions, he was repeatedly imprisoned by the British. He responded by engaging in hunger strikes that effectively created protest and sympathy for his cause.

In addition to his struggle for political independence, Gandhi fought to improve the status of the lowest classes of society, the casteless, or "Untouchables," whom he called *harijans* ("children of God"). When independence finally arrived in 1947, he opposed the splitting of the country into India and Pakistan, which was supposed to separate Muslims and Hindus to avoid their consistent fighting. Gandhi, for his part, wanted a more legitimate harmony for Hindus and Muslims, urging them to live together in peace. Ironically, in the end, he was assassinated not by a Muslim but by a Hindu fanatic.[16]

Sri Aurobindo (1872–1950)

Sri Aurobindo was a revolutionary, ascetic, patriot, philosopher, and yogi all rolled into one. Although he was a native of Calcutta, his father, Krishnadhan Ghose sent the boy abroad to study at St. Paul's school in London and King's College, Cambridge. In 1890, he returned to India and served in Baroda as a civil servant, a professor, and finally as vice-principal of Baroda College. By 1905, Aurobindo became enamored by the freedom struggle of India. His approach, however, was considered revolutionary for the time, as he encouraged direct political action instead of moderate reform. To convey his idea to others, he authored essays, poetry, dramas, and articles on nationalism, stirring India's political consciousness to action. He was soon appointed editor of the controversial *Bande Mataram* magazine and, developing a reputation as a political activist, was jailed for almost 1 year.

In prison he had a vision of Brahman, the all-pervading spiritual reality. This altered his mission in life, and, on being released from jail, he left politics aside. Instead, he retired to Pondicherry to pursue study, mysticism, and the mysteries of consciousness. In 1910, he established a temple and residence (*ashram*) there—The Aurobindo Ashram—and spent his time in meditation and in guiding disciples, who began to arrive in great numbers. This was largely a result of his many books and poetry, which he now wrote in profusion. Many of these books would later become famous.

Retiring in 1926, Aurobindo gave responsibility of the ashram to the "Mother," a French woman originally named Mirra Alfassa. Born in Paris in 1878 and arriving at Pondicherry in 1914, she continued his work until 1973, when she died. Before passing, however, she started many ambitious projects, which thrive to this day. For example, in 1953, she created the Sri Aurobindo International Educational Center in Pondicherry and in 1968, the community of Auroville, located a few miles from Pondicherry.

Bhaktisiddhanta Sarasvati Thakur (1874–1937)

Born in the holy pilgrimage place of Jagannath Puri, India, Bhaktisiddhanta Sarasvati, known in childhood as Bimala Prasad, was a pure devotee from a young age and eventually was renowned throughout India as one of her greatest scholars. At the age of 7 years, he had memorized many hundreds of Sanskrit texts and could speak illuminating commentaries on each of them. By the time he was 25 years old, he had an impressive reputation as a scholar of Sanskrit, mathematics, and astronomy. In fact, it was his astronomical treatise, *Surya siddhanta,* which won him the title *Siddhanta Sarasvati* ("One who knows ultimate conclusions by the grace of the Goddess of Learning") in recognition of his incomparable learning. In 1905, he accepted spiritual initiation from a sage named Gaura Kishora dasa Babaji.

Bhaktisiddhanta Sarasvati's father was Bhaktivinoda Thakur, an important nineteenth-century religious reformer who reestablished the integrity of the Bengali Vaishnava tradition. This tradition, which focuses on Krishna as the Supreme Personality of Godhead, had fallen into disrepute, cheating scholars and pseudo practitioners had bastardized the once pure teaching of the Vaishnava sages. Bhaktivinoda corrected this by rediscovering holy places associated with the tradition, writing prodigiously on the philosophical underpinnings of Vaishnava Hinduism, translating ancient texts into regional languages and into English, and showing in his own life how a Vaishnava ideally behaves.

The son carried on his work in much the same way, but his scholarship and passion for his subject reached many hundreds of thousands if not millions throughout the subcontinent, arguably surpassing the reach of his illustrious father. On the death of Bhaktivinoda Thakur in 1914, Bhaktisiddhanta became editor of his father's journal, *Sajjana-toshani,* and founded the Bhagwat Press for the publication of classical Vaishnava literature. In 1918, he accepted the renounced order of life, receiving the title Srila Bhaktisiddhanta Sarasvati Goswami Maharaja. Soon after he organized the Gaudiya Math, a monastic institution with the mission of reestablishing Vaishnavism as the eternal, nonsectarian function of the soul—a universal religion at the core of all spiritual traditions. He managed to open 64 branches throughout the country and also to send disciples to Europe for missionary work. This work would culminate in the success of his most effective disciple, A. C. Bhaktivedanta Swami Prabhupada, who extended the Gaudiya Math by creating the International Society for Krishna Consciousness (ISKCON) and preaching Bhaktisiddhanta's message around the world.[17]

Ramana Maharshi (1879–1950)

Considered among the most important Hindu mystics in the "all is one" vein, Ramana Maharshi was born in the village of Tirucculi near Madurai in southern India. At birth, he was given the name Venkataraman. His father died when Maharshi was 12 years old and at that time he went to live with his uncle in Madurai, a holy place further south. Here he briefly attended American Mission High School, but when his thoughts turned to religion he lost interest in all secular knowledge afforded by mundane education.

In his seventeenth year, he attained enlightenment; it was as if he experienced the complete demise of the physical body while remaining in full consciousness. After this transformative event, he left home and gravitated to the sacred hill of Arunachala, a traditional holy place to which he clung, averring that it was specially imbued with an intense spirituality. A community of like-minded devotees soon formed around him, and there he taught a form of non-duality, asking his followers to try to understand their "oneness" with God by simple meditative techniques and a life of humility. His teaching promoted the vision that God was in everything and everyone, and, accordingly, he had the utmost respect for animals, plants, and the entire natural world.[18]

Sarvepalli Radhakrishnan (1888–1975)

An Indian philosopher, statesman, and renowned interpreter of Hindu tradition, Radhakrishnan was born near Madras, South India, into an orthodox priestly family. In addition, he was educated in Christian missionary institutions, exposing him to religious criticism of Hindu tradition early on, as well as introducing him to Western philosophy. His early training, with both Eastern and Western influences, he believed, led to a balanced view of life.

His importance for Hindu tradition goes beyond abstract philosophy; he was President of India (1962–1967), where he had a deep impact on the people. Still, a good portion of his life was spent as a scholar; he was a philosophy professor at both Mysore and Calcutta Universities and also, after going to England, was Professor of Eastern Religion and Ethics at Oxford University (1936–1952). He held many other important academic positions before his election as President of India.

Once in office, he sought to abolish class distinction and caste, at least as commonly understood. He promoted a modern form of Hinduism that attempted to reconcile the world's religions, showing a unifying thread that permeated all religious thought. He wrote prodigiously and was knighted in 1931.

Paramahamsa Yogananda (1893–1952)

Yogananda was born Mukunda Lal Ghose in Gorakhpur, India. He came to the United States in 1920, devoting more than 30 years to working with Americans interested in God-realization. He "became" Yogananda in 1914 when he received initiation from his teacher Sri Yukteshwar, who also gave him the religious title Paramahamsa ("Swanlike Soul") in 1935. Yogananda means "bliss through yoga, or union with God," and this is indeed what he tried to teach.

His methods involved a secret technique of meditation, which he called Kriya-yoga, and he founded the Self-Realization Fellowship, an organization meant to carry on this work after his demise. The fellowship, with headquarters in Los Angeles, still has numerous centers throughout the world.[19]

Vinoba Bhave (1895–1982)

Vinoba Bhave was an Indian nationalist and social reformer who, according to many, is Mahatma Gandhi's spiritual successor. He created the Bhoodan ("land gift") movement, wherein he would travel the subcontinent and ask those who have multiple acres of land to donate a portion for equal distribution among the poor.

He was born in a Brahmin ("priestly") family in a small village just south of Bombay. In 1916, he began his spiritual quest, studying Sanskrit in earnest. But within 3 months he joined Gandhi's independence movement, viewing it mandatory that India win independence. Only then would her spiritual assets be recognized around the world. He learned Arabic and translated the Koran as a gesture to ensure Hindu-Muslim unity. Like Gandhi, he tirelessly crusaded for peace and understanding.

Jiddu Krishnamurti (1895–1986)

Annie Besant and C. W. Leadbeater, founding members of the Theosophical movement, met a young boy born of middle-class Brahmin parents, that is, from a priestly clan, and, although he was only 14 years old, recognized him as the coming world teacher. The boy was Jiddu Krishnamurti. The two theosophical stalwarts widely proclaimed the boy to be the reincarnation of both Christ and Buddha, and Besant adopted him and took him to England, where he was educated and groomed for his coming role.

Earlier, in 1889, Helena (Madame) Blavatsky, founder of the Theosophical Society, had told certain of her students that the purpose of theosophy was to prepare for the coming of a new Prophet, a World Teacher for the Aquarian Age. After Blavatsky's death, Annie Besant and C. W. Leadbeater made it their primary task to carry on this work, part of which was preparation for the coming Messiah.

Having found Krishnamurti, Besant and Leadbeater gave him intensive training in spiritual matters and a decade of special schooling in England. Soon, at age 27, Krishnamurti had an inner vision convincing him of his destined role. Theosophists the world over had been anticipating this development. Besant, especially, traveled throughout England and the United States with her protégé, announcing the arrival of the new Messiah.

In 1929, however, at the conclusion of this 2-year tour, Krishnamurti himself rejected all claims that he was the expected World Leader, and he disbanded the "World Order of the Star," a religious organization he had founded in 1911 to proclaim his Messiahship. Krishnamurti also renounced his association with the Theosophical Society at this point, although he maintained an active career of lecturing and writing. He finally settled in California, where, from 1969 until his death, he managed the Krishnamurti Foundation. His books remain a testimony to his wisdom and honesty.

Srila A.C. Bhaktivedanta Swami Prabhupada (1896–1977)

Born Abhay Charan De in Calcutta, India, Srila A.C. Bhaktivedanta Swami Prabhupada was raised from his early childhood as a pure devotee of Radha and Krishna, the female and male manifestations of Divinity. His father, Gaura Mohan, and his mother, Rajani, were both devoted to Radha and Krishna as well.

In early life he was a follower of Mahatma Gandhi; he was a married man with several children, and a chemist by profession, but he always longed to give his life to the Lord with heart and soul.

After an education at Scottish Church College, where he studied English, business, and philosophy—courses that would be useful when he eventually came to the United States to found ISKCON—he first met his spiritual master, Srila Bhaktisiddhanta Sarasvati Thakur in Calcutta in 1922. Bhaktisiddhanta, a prominent religious personality and the founder of 64 Gaudiya Mathas (Vedic institutes of knowledge), immediately marked this educated young man as a sincere soul. Accordingly, at their first meeting, he convinced him to dedicate his life to teaching Vedic knowledge—not Hinduism as a sectarian religion but as the eternal function of the soul, as a universal religion that elucidates the science of spirituality. Not only that, Bhaktisiddhanta specifically asked him to convey these teachings to the English-speaking world. Eleven years later, De became Bhaktisiddhanta's formally initiated disciple. A few years after that, Bhaktisiddhanta died.

De never forgot their first meeting or the few that took place after that. On each occasion Bhaktisiddhanta had asked him to broadcast Vedic knowledge in the English language. In the years that followed, in pursuance of that order, De had written a commentary on the Bhagavad Gita (an essential religious scripture), assisted Bhaktisiddhanta's institution in its missionary work, and, in 1944, started *Back to Godhead,* an English magazine that conveyed Bhaktisiddhanta's nonsectarian spiritual message.

In 1950, he retired from both business and family life, devoting more time to his studies and writing. To do this in an appropriate atmosphere, he traveled to the holy region of Braj, where Krishna had graced the earth some 5,000 years earlier. There he lived in humble circumstances, preparing himself for his journey West, to fulfill the order of his spiritual master. Soon, in 1959, he accepted the renounced order of life and was given the name A. C. Bhaktivedanta Swami. At the same time he began work on his life's masterpiece: a multi-volume translation and commentary of the 18,000-verse Shrimad-Bhagavatam (also known as the Bhagavata Purana). He was soon to write many such classics, but not before a long, arduous journey to the United States in September 1965.

After a year of great difficulty, he established the International Society for Krishna Consciousness in New York in July 1966. His movement blossomed beyond his wildest dreams, bearing the fruits that Bhaktisiddhanta and his many predecessors had prayed for. Appropriately, his disciples conferred on him the title Prabhupada, "the master at whose feet all other masters sit." Before he died on November 14, 1977, he had lovingly guided his Society and watched it grow to a worldwide confederation of more than 100 temples, schools, educational institutes, book publishing concerns, restaurants, and farm communities.[20]

Rukmini Devi Arundale (1904–1986)

Rukmini Devi Arundale is renowned as a teacher of Indian classical dance and as founder of Kalakshetra (Madras), an educational institution focusing on music, dance, fine arts, and crafts. Her interests expanded beyond these concerns, however, and she championed not only the cause of human rights but also the plight of animals. It was she who instigated a bill for the prevention of cruelty to animals and the establishment of the Animal Welfare Board. She also brought the first Montessori school to India.

Ahadevi Verma (1907–1987)

Ahadevi Verma is often considered one of India's greatest Hindi poets. Her publications include *Nihar* (1930), *Rashmi* (1932), *Sandhya Geet* (1936), and *Deepshika* (1942). Born in Farukhabad, Uttar Pradesh, she distinguished herself in a male-dominated society with an M.A. in Sanskrit and considerable knowledge of literature and holy texts. She was also an innovator in the field of education and served as principal of the Prayag Mahila Vidyapeeth, an important school in North India.

Swami Muktananda (1908–1982)

A controversial religious enthusiast from early in life, Muktananda quickly gained recognition for his mystical attainments. However, his real spiritual journey, he often said, was really sparked by his receiving *shakti-pat*, spiritual initiation, from Bhagawan Nityananda, a holy man for whom he had the deepest admiration. It was at this time, he claims, that his spiritual energy, or *kundalini,* was fully awakened, allowing for profound states of meditation.

In the 1970s, on his teacher's behalf, Muktananda brought the tradition to the West, giving the questionable *shaktipat* initiation to many thousands of spiritual seekers. He further established Gurudev Siddha Peeth as a public trust in India and founded the SYDA Foundation in the United States to administer the global work of Siddha Yoga meditation, as he came to call his particular path. Siddha Yoga basically means "the perfection of yoga."

Although he died in 1982, Swami Muktananda left the world many books on his peculiar version of Hindu thought and established more than 600 meditation centers around the world. In May 1982, he appointed two successors, Swami Chidvilasananda, and her brother, Swami Nityananda. Three years later, in October 1985, Nityananda resigned from the guru's role, with much debate about his reasons why. Swami Chidvilasananda then became the exclusive leader of the Siddha Yoga lineage. She continues her service to Swami Muktananda by sharing his spiritual legacy with the world through her lifestyle, travels, and words.[21]

Maharishi Mahesh Yogi (ca. 1917–)

Not much is known about Mararishi Mahesh Yogi's youth except that he was born in central India. He studied physics at Allahabad University and after receiving his degree he became a disciple of Swami Brahmananda Saraswati, the "Shankaracharya" (a follower of Adi Shankara) at Jyotir Math, in the Himalayas.

Maharishi refers to his teacher as "Gurudev," which is common nomenclature for holy teachers in India. The word means, "Divine Master." After Gurudev's death in 1953, Maharishi relocated in Uttar Kashi, in the high northern part of the Ganges. After 2 years of deep meditation in that part of the country, he felt an inner calling to travel to Rameshvaram, a holy city in the southernmost region of India.

While he was in the south, he began to formulate his own unique version of transcendental meditation. Although it was in essence the same technique taught to him by his master, he restructured it for a modern audience. Within a short time he found himself teaching this to thousands of people. In the years that followed, Maharishi traveled around the world teaching transcendental meditation (now referred to as TM) to anyone who approached him. The sheer numbers who did so were so overwhelming that, in 1960, he started training teachers and conceived a special Meditation Academy in Rishikesh, in the Himalayas. He soon initiated a plan to open TM centers in every major city in the world and eventually did so. He also encouraged scientific research into his TM technique and held conferences with various professionals—educators, administrators, businessmen, and so on—eventually making TM a household phrase.

In 1976, he introduced the TM-Sidhi course, which consists of advanced techniques for those who are somewhat accomplished in his technique. Then, in the 1980s, he founded Maharishi University of Management in Iowa, as well as other educational and research facilities. During the last two decades, Maharishi has revived other aspects of traditional Hindu knowledge, such as Ayurveda (holistic medicine), Sthapatya Veda (Hindu architecture), and Gandharva Veda (traditional Hindu music). He lives and has his headquarters in Vlodrop, The Netherlands.

Agehananda Bharati (1923–1991)

Agehananda Bharati was born Leopold Fischer in Vienna, Austria, and early on learned how to speak Hindi and associated dialects. He soon augmented this knowledge of Indian languages with his studies of classical Sanskrit. His first loves were Indian philosophy and culture and traveling around the world. His inborn taste for both, in fact, brought him to India, where he became a novice in a Hindu monastery. In time, he was initiated into the Dashanami Sannyasi order of Hindu monks. At that time, Fischer became Agehananda Bharati.

Bharati was both a monk and a teacher in a formal academic setting. His fields of interest included cultural anthropology, South Asian studies, linguistics, and comparative philosophy; and he taught courses in each of these at Delhi University, Banaras Hindu University, and the Nalanda Institute in India. He also taught in a Buddhist Academy in Bangkok, Thailand, where he started a popular course on comparative religion. He became a visiting professor of Indian philosophy in the University of Tokyo and Kyoto, as well. In 1956, he came to the United States as a research associate for Washington University. A year later he transferred to Syracuse University and joined the anthropology faculty there, where he eventually became the Ford-Maxwell Professor of South Asian Studies and, then, the department chairperson.

By the time of his death, Bharati had published more than 500 books and articles, including his now famous autobiography, *The Ochre Robe.*[22]

Mata Amritanandamayi Devi (1953–)

Amritanandamayi was born with the name Sudhamani in the small village of Parayakadavu, near Kollam, Kerala, in South India. Famous throughout the Hindu world as "Amma," or "Ammachi," or simply "Mother," she is a revered saint and as a tireless humanitarian.

Coming from simple, low-caste origins, she was schooled only until the age of 9, at which point she devoted all her time to providing for her family. She is a devotee of Krishna, the Supreme Godhead, and has been since her earliest years, when she had numerous mystical experiences. Her passion for spirituality blossomed into a love for all humanity, and, from her humble beginnings, her mission has grown to where she now addresses huge assemblies of tens of thousands around the world.

She founded a worldwide organization, the Mata Amritanandamayi Mission Trust, which focuses on spiritual and charitable welfare work. She now has a great number of disciples in all major regions of the world and well wishers who support her work; her contagious love is said to affect all who come into contact with her.

In 1993, she was one of the three people who represented Hinduism at the Parliament of the World's Religions in Chicago, echoing the work of Swami Vivekananda 100 years earlier. Amma was also the keynote speaker at The Global Peace Initiative of Women Religious and Spiritual Leaders, at the United Nations (UN) in Geneva, Switzerland. The UN conference was held in 2002 as part of the UN Millennium World Peace Summit, at which Amma spoke in August 2000.

She was recently presented with the Gandhi-King Award for nonviolence by The World Movement for Nonviolence at the UN General Assembly Hall (Palais Des Nations) in Geneva in recognition of her work in furthering the principles of nonviolence.

NOTES

1. Vidya Dehejia, *Antal and Her Path of Love* (Albany: SUNY Press, 1990).

2. John Carman, *The Theology of Ramanuja* (New Haven, CT: Yale University Press, 1974).

3. Deepak Sarma, *An Introduction to Madhva Vedanta* (Hampshire, England: Ashgate Publishing, 2003).

4. Richard Barz, *The Bhakti Sect of Vallabhacarya* (New Delhi: Munshiram Manoharlal, 1992).

5. Steven J. Rosen, "Who Is Shri Chaitanya Mahaprabhu?" in Edwin F. Bryant and Maria L. Ekstrand, eds., *The Hare Krishna Movement: The Postcharismatic Fate of a Religious Transplant* (New York: Columbia University Press, 2004), pp. 63–72.

6. Steven J. Rosen, *The Six Goswamis of Vrindavan* (New York: FOLK Books, 1992).

7. John Stratton Hawley, *Sur Das: Poet, Singer, Saint* (Seattle: University of Washington Press, 1984).

8. Http://www.sscnet.ucla.edu/southasia/Religions/gurus/Mirabai. html. See also Shama Futehally, *In the Dark of the Heart, Songs of Meera* (San Francisco: HarperCollins, 1994).

9. See John R. Hinnells, ed., *Who's Who of World Religions* (New York: Simon & Schuster, 1991), p. 342.

10. Raymond Brady Williams, *An Introduction to Swaminarayan Hinduism* (Cambridge: Cambridge University Press, 2001).

11. John R. Hinnells, ed., *Who's Who of World Religions* (New York: Simon & Schuster, 1991), pp. 96–97.

12. Romain Rolland, *The Life of Ramakrishna* (Calcutta: Advaita Ashrama, 1986). See also Jeffrey J. Kripal, *Kali's Child* (Chicago: The University of Chicago Press, 1998).

13. Shukavak Dasa, *Hindu Encounter with Modernity* (Los Angeles: Sri Publications, 1999).

14. See Tony K. Stewart and Chase Twichell, trans., *Rabindranath Tagore, The Lover of God* (Washington, DC: Copper Canyon Press, 2003).

15. John R. Hinnells, ed., *Who's Who of World Religions*, pp. 432–433.

16. Bart Gruzalski, *On Gandhi* (Belmont, CA.: Wadsworth/Thomson Learning, Inc., 2001). See also Catherine Clement, *Gandhi: The Power of Pacifism* (New York: Harry N. Abrams, 1996).

17. Rupa Vilasa Dasa, *A Ray of Vishnu* (Washington, MS: New Jaipur Press, 1988).

18. See A.L. Herman, *A Brief Introduction to Hinduism* (Boulder, CO: Westview Press, 1991).

19. See Paramahamsa Yogananda, *Autobiography of a Yogi* (Los Angeles: Self Realization Fellowship, 1998 reprint).

20. Satsvarupa Dasa Goswami, *Prabhupada: He Built a House in Which the Whole World Can Live* (Los Angeles: The Bhaktivedanta Book Trust, 1983).

21. See Brooks, et al., *Meditation Revolution: A History and Theology of the Siddha Yoga Lineage* (Hurleyville, NY: Agama Press, 1997).

22. Alfonso Narvaez, "Prof. A. Bharati, 68, a Monk Who Served on Syracuse Faculty." *The New York Times* (1991), p. 481. Also see Agehananda Bharati, *The Ochre Robe* (London: George Allen & Unwin, 1961).

GLOSSARY

Advaita: School of Hindu thought in which each living being is understood to be in some sense God. The chief characteristic of the school is its insistence on God's formlessness.

Ahimsa: Nonaggression and non-injury, a way of showing love to all creatures. This includes the idea of the sacredness of all life and its concomitant universal compassion. It is often extended to vegetarianism.

Asanas: Sitting and standing postures that aid in yogic exercise.

Avatar: Literally, "the Lord's descent." It refers to God's "incarnation" in the material world.

Ayurveda: Hindu system of holistic medicine and naturopathic healing.

Bhakti: Literally, "devotion." It refers to the moods and sentiments one may have for God.

Brahmacharis: Celibate students, usually young boys.

Brahmin: Intellectual or priestly caste in India.

Dashanami Sannyasi: Any renounced monk who is affiliated with the lineage of Shankara, the eighth-century teacher associated with this philosophical perspective.

Demigod: When God does not manifest in all His fullness, He is known as a demigod, literally, "half-god."

Dharma: "To support, hold up, or bear." In common parlance it means "right way of living," "Divine Law," "path of righteousness," "faith," and "duty." It refers to the essence of religion.

Dhoti: Single cloth male devotees where in place of pants.

Ekadashi: Fasting day that falls regularly on the eleventh day after the new moon and after the full moon as well.

Gaudiya Mathas: Vedic institutes of knowledge, particularly as defined by Bengali Vaishnavas. In the 1920s, a distinct organization by this name was inaugurated by the highly revered devotee and scholar, Srila Bhaktisiddhanta Sarasvati Thakur.

Ghee: Clarified butter

Gita: Literally, "song." It is usually used to refer to the Bhagavad Gita, the philosophical poem embedded in the Mahabharata.

Goloka: Lord Krishna's holy abode in the spiritual sky, the highest portion of Heaven. The earthly counterpart is known as Gokula, which can be found in the sacred area of Braj, Uttar Pradesh, India.

Grihasthas: Married devotees.

Guru: Teacher, usually of spiritual matters, but also used more generally.

Gurudev: Divine master, specifically for spiritual subjects.

Gyana: "Knowledge." Phonetic approximation of the more properly spelled *jnana.*

ISKCON: Acronym for the International Society for Krishna Consciousness, the modern-day Vaishnava movement that has spread the chanting of Krishna's names around the world.

Japa: Soft chanting of God's names, usually on rosary-type beads.

Jati: Literally, "birth." It refers to the modern-day caste system, wherein birth considerations are prominent in determining one's social station in life.

Karma: Work. The law of causality. Action and reaction.

Kirtan: Sacred art of chanting aloud.

Kshatriya: Administrative class; an officer of the law.

Kundalini-yoga: Form of mysticism involving the energy centers of the body. Often associated with the elevation of sexual energy.

Kurta: Long, collarless shirts worn by most Hindu men.

Mahotsava: Large festival.

Mantra: Sacred sound vibration, usually intended to bring one closer to God.

Masoretic text: Impeccable, hand-copied Hebrew text handed down by the Massoretes, a group of scribes who devised reliable means for preserving scriptures.

Maya: Illusion. The mistaking of one thing for another. Maya is usually identified with all things material, as opposed to that which is spiritual. It is also identified with the Goddess, whose domain is the material world.

Prabhupada: Honorific reserved for the best among spiritual teachers. Historically, the title is associated with Rupa Goswami Prabhupada and Bhaktisiddhanta Sarasvati Thakur Srila Prabhupada, among others. In the modern era, it is primarily known as the name of His Divine Grace A.C. Bhaktivedanta Swami Prabhupada.

Pranayama: Breath control associated with yogic mysticism.

Prasadam: Literally, "mercy." Vegetarian food sanctified by prayers and ritualistic offerings.

Puja: Literally, "worship." It refers chiefly to the systematic worship of deities, or iconic forms, in temples or in Hindu homes.

Raja-yoga: Path of using physical exercise, sitting postures, and meditation to gain closeness with the Supreme. Because the Raja-yoga system is described in eight steps, it is sometimes called Ashtanga-yoga, "the eightfold path," but it is more commonly known as Hatha-yoga.

Rama Rajya: Kingdom of Rama, the incarnation of Vishnu. The term is now used to refer to any righteous rule.

Rashtriya Panchang: Religious calendar.

Sampradaya: "Lineage." Hindu groups are divided into specific sects with teachings and traditions that vary. Each is called a particular *sampradaya*, such as the Gaudiya Sampradaya or the Vallabha Sampradaya, usually based on the name of the systematizer of a particular lineage or a distinct teaching that separates that lineage from another.

Samskaras: Sacraments.

Sanatana Dharma: "Eternal Duty." Nature of the soul, divorced from mundane misconceptions and worldly illusions.

Sankirtan: Sacred art of chanting performed congregationally.

Sannyasis: Renounced order of life. Celibate, elderly monks who live only for service to God.

Sari: Cloth worn by women in traditional India.

Satya-yuga: First of the world ages in the Hindu tradition. After Satya comes Treta-yuga, and then Dvapara and Kali. Each of the ages is progressively shorter in duration, as are the longevity and qualifications of those who live in them.

Shiva Lingam: Aniconic form of Lord Shiva representing the creative force of the universe. Depicted as his genitalia, it symbolizes the generative ability of God and the procreative magic of the universe.

Shruti: "Revelation." The earliest portion of Hinduism's sacred texts.

Shudra: Worker. who is suited to helping the three higher castes.

Sri/Srila: "Auspicious" or "beauty." Often used as a term of respect.

Sthapatya Veda: Hindu architecture.

Supersoul: Indwelling God. Vishnu, as he pervades each individual soul and each atom of the universe.

Surya Siddhanta: Text dealing with astronomy and astrological sciences.

Swami: "Controller of one's sense." A title for accomplished masters.

Tantric: Scriptural guidelines. Often connected with sexual practices leading to enlightenment.

Tapas: Penance and austerity.

Tilak: Generally thought of as sectarian markings distinguishing one Hindu group from another. Vaishnavas see these markings as energy centers for the soul and as eternal symbols of their devotion to Vishnu.

Tithis: Literally "day." It is the thirtieth part of the lunar month.

Tulasi: Plant, in the basil family that is especially dear to Lord Krishna. The plant is considered an incarnation of Vrinda, a divine cowherd girl. Accordingly, devotees wear beads made of *tulasi* wood, show great veneration to her in daily services, and consume her leaves when she leaves her plantlike body.

Vaishya: Mercantile class and those adept at commerce, for example, traders and farmers.

Vanaprastha: Stage of life just before total renunciation, wherein one retires from the rigors of worldly life and starts to devote full time to spiritual matters.

Varnashrama: Social system considered essential in the proper and effective functioning of humankind. Varnashrama is ideally based on intrinsic quality and natural aptitude as opposed to birthright.

Vedas: Hinduism's earliest sacred texts.

Vraja (or Braj): Land of Lord Krishna. There is a celestial Braj and an earthly Braj, and devotees see them as the same.

Yoga: From the Sanskrit root *yuj*, which means "to link up with, to combine." It refers not only to physical exercises but also to various religious paths described in the Hindu scriptures.

Yogis: Those who practice yoga.

Yugas: World cycles of Hindu history.

SELECTED BIBLIOGRAPHY

GENERAL HINDUISM

Flood, Gavin. *An Introduction to Hinduism*. New York: Cambridge University Press, 1996.

Flood, Gavin, ed. *The Blackwell Companion to Hinduism*. Oxford, UK: Blackwell Publishing, 2003.

Huyler, Steven P. *Meeting God: Elements of Hindu Devotion*. New Haven, CT: Yale University Press, 1999.

Klostermaier, Klaus K. *A Survey of Hinduism*. 2nd ed. Albany: State University of New York Press, 1994.

Michaels, Axel. *Hinduism: Past and Present*. Princeton, NJ: Princeton University Press, 2004.

Mittal, Sushil, and Gene Thursby, eds. *The Hindu World*. New York: Routledge, 2004.

DENOMINATIONS

Vaishnavism

Bryant, Edwin F. *Krishna: The Beautiful Legend of God*. New York: Penguin Classics, 2003.

Chakravarti, Sudhindra Chandra. *Philosophical Foundation of Bengal Vaishnavism*. Calcutta, India: Academic Publishers, 1969.

Narayanan, Vasudha. *The Vernacular Veda*. Columbia: University of South Carolina Press, 1994.

Prabhupada, A. C. Bhaktivedanta Swami. *The Science of Self-Realization*. Los Angeles: The Bhaktivedanta Book Trust, 1977.

Rosen, Steven J., ed. *Vaisnavism: Contemporary Scholars Discuss the Gaudiya Tradition*. Delhi, India: Motilal Banarsidass Publishers, 1994, reprint.

Shaivism

Danielou, Alain. *Gods of Love and Ecstasy: The Traditions of Shiva and Dionysus*. Rochester, VT.: Inner Traditions International, 1994.

Dehejia, Harsha V. *Parvatidarpana: An Exposition of Kasmir Saivism through the Images of Siva and Parvati*. New Delhi, India: Motilal Banarsidass, 1999.

Mishra, Kamalakar. *Kashmir Shaivism: The Central Philosophy of Tantrism*. Cambridge, UK: Rudra Press, 1993.

O'Flaherty, Wendy Doniger. *Siva, the Erotic* Ascetic. New York: Oxford University Press, 1981.

Smith, David. *The Dance of Siva: Religion, Art and Poetry in South India*. Cambridge: Studies in Religious Traditions, No 7, Cambridge University Press, 1996.

Subramuniyaswami, Satguru Sivaya. *Dancing with Siva: Hinduism's Contemporary Catechism*. Concord, CA: Himalayan Academy, 1993.

Shaktism

Hawley, John Stratton, and Donna Marie Wulff, eds. *Devi: Goddesses of India*. Berkeley: University of California Press, 1996.

Johnsen, Linda. *Daughters of the Goddess: The Women Saints of India*. Saint Paul, MN: Yes International Publishers, 1994.

Kinsley, David. *Hindu Goddesses*. Los Angeles: University of California Press, 1986.

Kripal, Jeffrey J. *Kali's Child*. Chicago: The University of Chicago Press, 1998.

Kurtz, Stanley N. *All the Mothers Are One: Hindu India and the Cultural Reshaping of Psychoanalysis*. New York: Columbia University Press, 1992.

Pintchman, Tracy. *The Rise of the Goddess in the Hindu Tradition*. Albany: State University of New York Press, 1994.

RESOURCE GUIDE

Websites

http://www.hindunet.org/ (contains "The Hindu universe," a comprehensive resource guide to all things Hindu).
http://www.hindulinks.org/
http://www.krishna.com
http://www.hinduwebsite.com/

Periodicals

Hinduism Today
www.hinduismtoday.com
Back to Godhead
P. O. Box 430
Alachua, FL 32616
Phone: 800–800–3284
E-mail: editors@krishna.com

International Journal of Hindu Studies
c/o International Institute of India Studies
1270 St-Jean
St-Hyacinthe
Quebec
Canada J2S 8M
Phone: 514–771–02

Journal of Vaishnava Studies
c/o Deepak Heritage Books
P. O. Box 2130
Poquoson, VA 23662
Phone: 757–766–5830
E-mail: dhb@stcnet.com

Publishers

South Asia Books,
P. O. Box 502
Columbia, MO 65205
Phone: 573–474–0116
E-mail: sabooks@juno.com

The Bhaktivedanta Book Trust
P. O. Box 34074
Los Angeles, CA 90034
Phone: 800–927–4152
E-mail: BBTUSA@krishna.com

Art

Mandala Publishing Group
2240-B 4th Street
San Rafael, CA 94901
Phone: 415–460–6112
www.mandala.org

Organizations

Self-Realization Fellowship
3880 San Rafael Avenue, Dept. 9W
Los Angeles, CA
Phone: 323–225–2471
www.yogananda-srf.org

Ramakrishna-Vivekananda Center of New York
17 East 94th Street
New York, NY 10128
Phone: 212–534–9445
www.ramakrishna.org

The International Society for Krishna Consciousness
(ISKCON)
3764 Watseka Avenue
Los Angeles, CA 90034
Phone: 310–836–2676
www.harekrishnala.com
www.iskcon.com

Film

ITV Productions
Phone: 310–455–8968
www.itvproductions.net

INDEX

Boldface numbers refer to volume numbers: 1: Judaism; 2: Confucianism and Taoism; 3: Buddhism; 4: Christianity; 5: Islam; 6: Hinduism.

About the Authors

EMILY TAITZ is an independent scholar and author of *The Jews of Medieval France: The Community of Champagne* (Greenwood, 1994) and numerous essays on Judaism and the coauthor of *Remarkable Jewish Women: Rebels, Rabbis and Other Women from Biblical Times to the Present* (2002), among other works.

RANDALL L. NADEAU is Associate Professor of East Asian Religions at Trinity University, San Antonio, Texas.

JOHN M. THOMPSON teaches in the Department of Philosophy and Religious Studies, Christopher Newport University, Newport News, Virginia.

LEE W. BAILEY is Associate Professor of Philosophy and Religion at Ithaca College.

ZAYN R. KASSAM is Associate Professor of Religious Studies and Chair of the Religious Studies Department, Pomona College.

STEVEN J. ROSEN is an independent scholar and prolific writer on Hinduism.